THE LAST EMPIRE

A SHORT HISTORY OF TWENTIETH CENTURY RUSSIA

JEEVA PITCHAIMANI

XpressPublishing
An imprint of Notion Press

No.8, 3rd Cross Street,CIT Colony,
Mylapore, Chennai, Tamil Nadu-600004

ISBN 978-1-64919-246-2

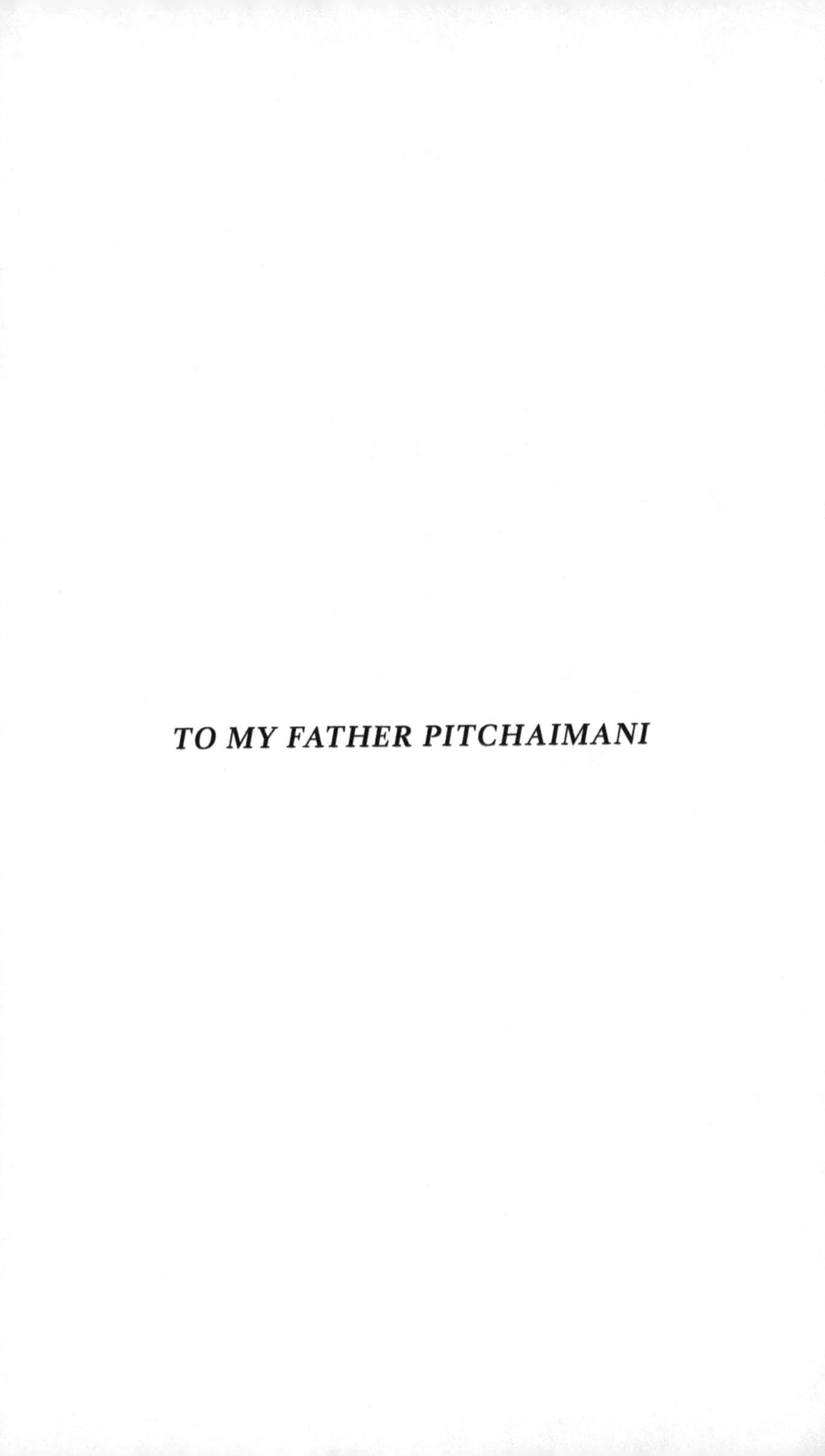

TO MY FATHER PITCHAIMANI

Contents

Contents

Foreword

This book was originally intended as a cheap imitation of my icon Pandit Jawaharlal Nehru's masterpieces - Glimpses of World History and the Discovery of India. Right from my childhood, the subject of history has always served as a source of fascinating stories and events for me as a result of which I was able to cultivate a deep love for the subject regardless of the difficulties it posed as an examination subject. Nehru's work in history I felt, was seminal in making the subject accessible and inspiring to readers of every shade which he had achieved by imbuing the events with fine human touches and interesting literary allusions.

I have tried hard in these pages to do away almost completely with the pedantic approach to writing history that focusses too much on dates, events and names. All that matters here for me is the story, its philosophical dimensions, the human angles and the impact it had on the lives of people and their thoughts. Hence the tale might look more like historical fiction, a calm recounting of events than a scholarly treatise on historical events that took place in Russia.

Before I start with my story, I would like to come clean on my ideological biases that inform the rest of the pages. I belong to the left-wing of the political spectrum though I am no politician. I am deeply in love with Marxism and its currents though the same cannot be said about my relationship with the Marxists. To put it in another way, I do not pretend to give an unbiased or an objective view of Russian history through this book.

If it is not going to be scholarly, if it is not going to be objective why you may wonder should you read this book?

The book in the first place has been written with nothing more than a primal concern for the contemporary human condition. The only idea which I strongly believe shall liberate humanity from the clutches of exploitation and poverty is Marxism and Soviet Russia was the first country in the world to form a government founded on its principles. But the Marxist idea instead of liberating Russians from its oppressors, to everyone's shock and disappointment began to devour lives and livelihoods ruthlessly, not in hundreds or thousands but in millions.

But instead of overthrowing such a ruthless government at the earliest opportunity they had, the Russians curiously persisted with it. In fact, they came out in hordes in support of it and laid their lives to defend it. Just when the rest of the world thought that the foolish Russians were doomed once and for all, they rose stirringly backed by their government and competed superbly with better-placed nations and superpowers. At some point in time, it was apparent to the rest of the world that the government of the empire had mysteriously lost all its predatory instincts and was working towards transforming the lives of its citizens for the better with sincerity and commitment.

As the rest of the world had gotten used to the state of affairs that had increasingly been dominated by Russia and its powerful influence, the empire defying expectations once again, began to break up. It disintegrated rapidly confounding both its supporters and detractors and one final day committed an unexpected harakiri. From that day on, the world could never remain the same place again.

Working people all over the world started finding themselves suddenly bereft of any moral support. The poor steadily grew poorer while the rich of the world hastily inherited the planet. The world, even if it was producing more and more at a rapid pace, even if it had managed to look opulent and sophisticated than ever before began to hide more than what it could honestly reveal. Glaring inequalities, racial and religious tensions, increasing number of diseases and ailments, rising levels of planetary temperature and frequent natural disasters had suddenly become the new normal in the world.

If one is not ready to accept my contention that Soviet Russia was at the heart of all these contemporary events, if one is ready to process unusual ideas with an open mind, my dear reader, I heartily welcome you into my pages.

Preface

...

Acknowledgements

When I began writing this book as a series of essays, if not for the help of the National Award-winning film critic Mr Baradwaj Rangan who helped me publish them in his blog, I would probably not have taken it to completion. I am deeply indebted to him not only on account of his help in getting this published but also for serving as a huge influence on me as a writer.

I would like to acknowledge the support given by my friends Vinodh Babu and Chandrasekar who kept giving me valuable feedback after completion of every chapter, almost instantly. I want to acknowledge the contribution of Naveen Kumar, my childhood buddy as well.

Special thanks to my alter-ego Arulmozhivarman who played a great role in keeping the flame in me alive.

Finally I would also like to thank my mother Latha Pitchaimani, an embodiment of sacrifice and resilience who has remained an unwavering pillar of support for me all these years, my wife Lavanya who has been a model wife ever since we knew each other and my little son Kadhirnilavan for whom this book I hope shall serve as a valuable education in the future.

Prologue

I was 10 years old then. It must have been a day in Summer 1998.

'Dad, why do you go to the Union Office and pay them every month?'

'It is a practice in the Communist Party, son. We workers will have to sacrifice a part of our wages so that the party survives.'

'So dad, you mean your party is poor?'

'Yes.'

'Why do you have to belong to a party that is poor? Why don't you join a rich party, dad?'

'I am a Unionist. My Union is affiliated to the Communist party. Communist parties are the only ones which work for the poor and the oppressed. Rich parties do not work for the poor'

'Why don't they work for the poor?'

'Son, Rich parties are rich because they are funded by rich people. Rich people, more often than not want only to become richer. They sponsor political parties and make them rich. Once the party becomes rich and captures power it will start working for them. The sponsors in turn get richer and they fund the rich party more. The cycle continues. All parties in India are rich parties. Only the Communist Party is funded by me, Clerk Varada Uncle, Auto Driver Govindan Uncle, Maran Master, Plumber Udhayakumar Uncle and so on. Poor and middle class people like us are the only ones who fund this party. Even Kerala CM is poor'

• • •

Must be ten years later. I was twenty years old then. 2008.

'Dad, people say the whole world is caught in a recession, all of a sudden one fine morning. Wasn't there anyone who could predict all this and stop before it got worse?'

'Only one person so far has predicted this and he is no longer alive'

'Oh great dad, Who?'

'Karl Marx, he predicted quite correctly how capitalism shall behave. Do you know there is a massive demand for Das Capital written by him now in Germany, nearly 150 years after it was published?

'Dad, so do you say Marxism shall cure the world of all its problems?'

'Definitely, son'

'Why did Russia relinquish Communism then?'

'A lot of reasons. People were selfish and wanted to earn quickly'

'Oh ok, dad. I wanted to ask why are you coming home early nowadays after office? All these days you always used to come not before 9 PM'

'I am no longer active in the Union. I was replaced in the Union by Suresh, my colleague you know'

'Oh. Why?'

'Lot of infighting. I also raised questions on the Communist Party's approach towards industrialisation in West Bengal. You heard about firings on locals in Singur and Nandigram? I told them that we will lose West Bengal if we continue like this. The Unit leadership was not happy that I spoke like this. They decided to replace me. So I stopped being active in the Union and the Party'.

• • •

It was 2018. My father had retired from his job.

'Dad did you look at the news that only 1 percent of the population in India owns more than 60 percent of India's wealth?'

'Yes. Laissez Faire Capitalism works like that'

'Wasn't India unequal like this before?'

'It wasn't this unequal. We embraced economic reforms in 1991. So our wealth distribution started to skew. We have more than half a million farmers dead due to State Negligence. Our State no longer is a Welfare State'

'Dad, I read somewhere that the concept of Welfare State arose in the West. So did India copy that?'

'Yes, the USSR seized all means of production from landowners and industrialists. The state controlled everything. Rich people in the West were afraid that if Communism spreads to their country, they may have to lose everything. So they combined elements of Soviet Communism with Capitalism and evolved something called Welfare State. It is also called a Mixed Economy. Nehru wanted to emulate that in India. He did with only moderate success.'

'Dad, so you mean to say that the collapse of the USSR went hand in hand with the world going back to Laissez Faire Capitalism?'

'Yes. That was one of the key reasons. Once there was no counterweight to the Free Market West in the form of the USSR, the West started spreading free market ideas to the Third-World like India. India wouldn't have probably embraced the Free Market had the USSR managed to live beyond 1991'.

• • •

A year later, 2019. A few days before I started writing this book.

'Dad, I am halfway through Pin Thodarum Nizhalin Kural by Jeyamohan. He has accused Stalin of killing millions of Russians. Why did Stalin do that? Isn't the idea of Marxism built on the idea of love, like how Kamal Haasan emphasised in Anbe Sivam?'

'Don't believe what the bourgeoisie writers say. They know nothing'

'Dad, he isn't a bourgeoisie. He was once a part of the Communist Party himself. You have told me many a time that Communists are honest people. Why does he have to lie?'

'You never know in the Communist Party. There may be bad people as well'

'And they may be killed as well by the Party itself, dad?'

'I am going for a walk. We will talk later'

'Dad, I want to know what really happened in the USSR. Why was Trotsky killed? Wasn't he one of the founders of the USSR? How could he be a bad person? Why was Bukharin killed?'

'You read too much of George Orwell I guess. This isn't good for you. Orwell was a traitor'

'Orwell joined the Communist Party but was expelled. He lived as a Communist throughout his life'

'People leave the party and pretend they are ideologically committed'

'Dad, who was Pol Pot?'

'He was a Cambodian dictator. He killed millions'

'He was a Communist, dad. Why don't you mention that?'

'He misused the name of Communism. But he was originally a dictator'

'If he was not a Communist, why did Communist China support him in his fight against Communist Vietnam?'

'You have grown up, son. I don't have anything to tell you'

'You gotta defend your Party. Come on, dad. We're just having a conversation'

'I am no longer part of the Party. I quit as soon as I retired from service'

'Oh what, why dad?'

'The Communist Party cannot be reformed. They are going to doom'

'I don't understand. On one issue, you speak as though the Party is infallible and anyone who talks against the Party is a traitor. On another, you say the Party is incorrigible. Why there is so much contradiction?'

'I will leave it to you to find that, son'.

THE INSTALLATION

CHAPTER I

The Installation

Contrary to what is generally assumed, Russia on the eve of the October Revolution was not a well-developed industrial country. It was not even imperialist, in the Western sense of the word and had no colonies in Africa or Asia or Latin America. Russia's impending defeat in the First World War towards the end of 1917, had squelched all national spirit, and a growing number of deserters in the army hampered even the slightest chance of a military recovery. The Tsars were bent on prolonging the war for their own survival reasons, but were shocked to witness mutinies, unrest and anarchy everywhere which to a substantial degree was the natural response to the centuries- old harsh and repressive regime that they had imposed upon their people. Russia, primarily an agricultural country had millions of poor peasants and a small, growing industrial proletariat. The despotic Tsar regime subjected the peasants to massive taxation which increased exponentially with the coming of the World War. Peasants desperately waited for a savior to emancipate them from all insufferable hardships and implicitly pinned their hopes on a lot of anti-monarchist movements that were growing here and there in Russia.

Revolution Underway:

One such movement was headed by the Russian Social Democratic Party (RSDLP) which was nothing but a group of left wing radicals united by a broad range of 19th century socialist ideals. The party had two prominent factions which nurtured divergent ideological visions of a future utopian society but had, fortunately decided to resolve their differences at a later point of time - after the overthrow of the implacable Tsarist monarchy.

One of the factions, the Bolsheviks was headed by Vladimir Lenin, a pragmatic Marxist, as he liked to call himself. The other, the Mensheviks, was headed by Alexander Kerensky a socialist radical who didn't approve of Marxism but was, nevertheless a very progressive revolutionary. The Bolsheviks promised ' Land, Peace and Bread' to the people and hence were able to command a wide and a lasting appeal among the masses. By early 1917 as the World War was drawing to a close, the Tsar, sensing popular unrest, abdicated the throne which gave way to the installation of a provisional Government led by Kerensky. People voted for the RSDLP as a whole but it was Kerensky who seized power as soon as he divined its proximity. Kerensky, the politically shrewd ruler as he was, expecting a backlash from Lenin in the immediate future, ordered for the elimination of the Bolsheviks through legal as well extra- legal measures. The power struggle ensued for several months but it was only on November 7 the same year that the Bolsheviks seized power under the leadership of the indefatigable Lenin.

Repercussions:

This takeover of power by Lenin, also called the Russian Revolution of 1917 marked a watershed moment in the global history of the 19th century. This was the first time ever that a government openly espousing Marxist ideals was formed in any country and the shudders it sent through the rest of the world cannot be underestimated. The Imperialist Western Europe was alarmed at the ascent of the Communists in the largest country of the world and for the first time in history the ruling classes increasingly felt that they had to confront something 'sceptral' in order to survive the near future. On the other hand, the victory of the Russian Revolution gave hope to millions of oppressed, poor and enslaved people in countries world over including colonies such as those of India. In every colony in Asia and Africa, local communists began to play the leading role in the national liberation struggle against the West European Imperialists.

A lot of European countries along with the US failed to recognize the Government of the Soviet Union led by Lenin which began to grow in size as other adjoining countries such as Kazakhstan, Armenia, Ukraine, etc also started acceding to the Communist Union. Most importantly the victory of the Bolsheviks inspired liberation struggle in the neighbouring China as well, which was also to become Communist in the next 30 years.

Intellectuals all over the world especially in Great Britain and even in the US felt that Russia had turned a new leaf over and expected their own countries to follow suit in order to attain a society devoid of exploitation, racism and religious fanaticism. The British Raj in India passed the Rowlatt Act of 1919 outlawing any form of protest against the Government so as to clampdown on the Indian Communists and its sympathizers. In various colonies, their respective governments banned their local Communist parties and a massive witch-hunting of communist radicals followed.

The massive land reform that the Bolshevik government had undertaken in Russia soon after its formation stripped the nobles and princes and landlords of their possessions and left them 'cold and hostile' to the proletarian establishment. They were waiting for an opportunity to pay back Lenin and his coterie, all the while despairing strongly for a restoration of the monarchy. For the dislodged

Russian ruling classes, soon help was to arrive in the form of Western aid.

The first challenge:

It was 1921 when Lenin's plans to revive a war ravaged country were slowly bearing fruit, though shortages and occasional famines occurred in the rural areas. In many ways, the effort was humongous and Lenin's leadership used both coercive as well as democratic means to involve people in this historic endeavour. People did find enormous reserves of patriotism and revolutionary spirit within themselves that they were ready to serve the Bolshevik government in any capacity as was required.

However, the dethroned ruling classes on the other hand, with substantial help from the Western powers were meticulously plotting for a counter revolution hell-bent on restoring Russia to its Tsarist days. Civil war broke out in 1918 which took Lenin by surprise and the bloody conflict between the Red Army and the counter revolutionaries began to hamper the rebuilding effort. The Bolsheviks managed to defeat the counter-revolutionaries after a prolonged battle which unwittingly ended up altering Lenin's attitude towards his people remarkably.

Lenin on no account, was willing to allow Russia tailspin into its pre-1917 era of darkness, as a result of which his revolutionary optimism started giving way to an over-cautiousness that was soon to transmogrify into a terrible paranoia. Lenin evolved something that was to be called 'War Communism' which meant a lot of things including elimination of inner party democracy and ruthless suppression of dissent. Freedom of speech and other basic freedoms were to be suspended 'for a while', during which the revolutionary government will succeed in obliterating any surviving relic of 'counter- revolution and reaction' that might potentially harm the country's 'historic march into socialism'. Trade unions were effectively weakened and the State decided to intrude into every aspect of its citizen's life so as to purge any reactionary tendencies or urges that were left inside him. Workers and peasants were mandated to stretch beyond their healthy limits and any attempt to stray out of the line was repulsed ruthlessly. Concentration camps which were initially set up to punish the erstwhile royalists and landlords for their past excesses, began to swell in size feeding upon innocent citizens and Communist dissidents as well. The party branched out into all the departments of governmental administration and the Soviet Union was slowly beginning to resemble a 'Police State' perennially vigilant and incurably paranoid about its security and existence.

The Soviet Union after surviving its first threat to life with a fair amount of success was to wake up to another one very shortly. Vladimir Lenin, the peerless revolutionary who united the whole of backward Russia under one banner, died prematurely in 1922 at the age of 54.

MAN OF STEEL

CHAPTER II

Twin Towers

The death of the founder patriarch Vladimir Lenin, did jolt the Soviet people even though it was very well known that he was bedridden for months. Lenin's New Economic Policy introduced in 1921 a few months before his death, had to a very considerable extent mollified the disenchanted people who had been deprived of their basic human rights. The NEP, as it was called, encouraged private ownership of land and market pricing of their grain which in turn provided the farmers with strong initiative to employ new methods of farming and increase production. The increased food production helped mitigate food shortages and famines which indirectly neutralised the rebellious instincts of the masses. People were slowly getting used to yet another form of authoritarian leadership but they still sincerely believed that better futures lay in store for them.

The death of Lenin, indeed had created a great vacuum at the highest level of the Soviet leadership and observers abroad were hurriedly drafting their celebratory obituaries for the short-lived revolution. Lenin during his last few years had preferred Josef Stalin, one of his close confidantes during the revolutionary years, to succeed him, but soon began to waver from his position for multiple reasons. Stalin was known to be ruthless and scheming during his stint with the government and had alienated a lot of party founders with his intolerant attitude. Leon Trotsky, another long-time associate of Lenin was a strong contender for the position of Lenin's successor.

Some more names were also in contention soon after Lenin's death which ultimately triggered an intense power struggle within the party.

Josef Stalin known for his skill in manipulation and political manoeuvring, finally emerged successful at the end of the struggle. Stalin, unlike his successors was a ruler who assumed power with a clear vision for Soviet Russia and hence in many ways served the primary purpose of consolidating Communist power over its vast, diverse landscape. Stalin, to start with, successfully solved the problem of multiple nationalities vying against one another for supremacy by implementing in practice with considerable success, Lenin's all-inclusive theory of nationalism. Many languages belonging to various communities were given preference in school curriculum as well in administrative affairs. The effectiveness of this policy in cementing the various nationalities into the broad Communist bloc cannot be underestimated.

'War Communism' introduced by Lenin only on an emergency basis, was institutionalised under Stalin and in fact, further intensified all over the Union. This doctrine with a few more inputs from Stalin came to be known as 'Marxism-Leninism'. Marx who envisioned 'collective form of property' for the Communist future believed only in an evolutionary form of societal development, which meant society relieving itself from the chains of feudalism, moving slowly into capitalism and concomitantly into a state of unsustainable inequality which in turn would pave the way for State Socialism finally culminating in what is known as Stateless Communism. Lenin too, during his time as a revolutionary, had analysed the Russian feudal conditions and theoretically dismissed the chances for a Communist Revolution in the country. Even Marx a few decades before Lenin, expected a Communist Revolution in the near future, only in a highly industrialised country like Germany or Britain and not certainly in a backward, underdeveloped and feudal Russia. But what happened in Russia in 1917 was a curious combination of factors that were milked to the extreme by a shrewd Marxist politician in Lenin, as a result of which the Communists came to power all over Eastern Europe.

Unite or be killed:

Stalin was too impatient to allow Russia to pass through its Marxist 'evolutionary' phases and hence decided to force Communism down the throats of the unwilling populace. Lands that were distributed by Lenin to peasants during the early days of the Soviet government, were decreed to be ceded to the State along with other private property. Farmers were totally unwilling to let the State take over their lands and possessions as a result of which there was a spike in the number of rebellions and unrests by late 1930s. These disturbances were ruthlessly suppressed by Stalin's powerful machinery and concentration camps in Siberia were allowed to burgeon towards unprecedented sizes. Secret police who came to be known as KGB later, roamed all over the country and any signs of dissent or protest were prematurely identified and suitably eliminated. Another group encouraged by Stalin was the Communist Youth League which was full of young 'radicals' whose main duty was assisting the police in weeding out dissent. Fear spread all over the country and people stopped discussing politics in public places fearing retribution.

However the most important outcome of collectivisation was a steep fall in agricultural output and rampant starvation and shortages all over the Union.

Farmers were not willing to toil for pittances and were indignant with the State for diverting a large portion of the agricultural output towards cities and industrial towns. Stalin right from the beginning was very anxious to build Russia's image for the West, as a rapidly industrialising country all set to overtake its capitalist competitors. Even though Stalin succeeded in industrialising Russia through steel and armament industries, the human and economic cost incurred was massive and largely avoidable. Ukraine lost almost 3 million people in 1933 to man-made famines and poverty. Stalin on the other hand was using everything in his power to sustain his image through State propaganda tools such as the radio and the press. Russia was portrayed to its people and outside as a nation on the cusp of a major Communist transformation, which polarised opinion in the depression-hit capitalist countries.

More about Russia's instrumental role in indirectly influencing the politics of other countries will be seen in the upcoming chapters.

Fascism and Russia:

Just like how Communist Russia was influencing the depression-hit Capitalist West, the rise of Hitler in Germany sent shudders throughout the world. Marxist historians rightly called 'Fascism' the most advanced stage of Laissez Faire Capitalism where all relics of bourgeois liberalism and democracy are blown to smithereens. Hitler strongly polarised opinions all over the world leading to fascist movements in Spain, Poland, Japan etc. Fascism in Europe was thoroughly anti-Semitic and Jews all over the world were viewed with suspicion and fear. Blacks in the US were similarly ill-treated especially when the economic depression was at its peak.

People all over the recession-hit countries started looking for economic alternatives both in Germany and Russia. People stopped believing in parliamentary democracy and waited for the emergence of strong, charismatic leaders and individuals who could make decisions on their own. This was also the time when Communist Parties in Western countries began to gather enormous mass support and therefore threatened the electoral hegemony of the hitherto dominant centrist forces. These Communist parties were part of a Communist International led by the Russian Communist Party (Lenin's faction of the RSDLP became the Russian Communist Party in 1918) and directly reported to Josef Stalin in various periodic conferences. The political lines to be adopted in their respective countries were dictated by Stalin and his coterie, and any deviation by the domestic leadership was dealt with severely. As a result, these parties sang paeans to Communist Russia and its industrial achievements and promised people with a radical left wing alternative to all their economic problems.

Russia, in turn led the anti-Fascist bloc while the Soviet press vilified Hitler and his policies keeping people aware of the ever-present threat of fascism. When liberal democratic leaders in various countries like Britain, US and France were trying to appease Hitler and moderate his ambitions, Stalin's Russia kept showing a virtual middle finger to the Fascist bloc. Stalin was continuously sending feelers to the Western countries to form an official United Front against Hitler but was snubbed time and again. Intellectuals all over the world were impressed with the theoretical soundness of Marxist analysis of Fascism and were impelled to join newly mushrooming Fascist Resistance movements in their respective countries. In many ways, the fact that Communists and left wing radicals spearheaded the International Resistance movements against fascism is beyond doubt.

A Spanish debacle:

In 1936, a broad left wing coalition government headed by the Spanish Communists won the elections in Spain. Fearing communist expansion to other neighbouring areas, Hitler helped the Spanish General Francisco Franco to stage a military coup against the democratically elected government. The military coup was successful and a fascist government under Franco was about to be installed. This triggered protests all over Spain and the rest of the world which soon transformed into what was known as the Spanish Civil War of 1936. The Spanish Communist party, the Trotskyist party (POUM) along with other left wing parties at one end (known as Republicans) supported by thousands of civilians from across the world and the Spanish Nationalist Army supported by Hitler and Mussolini at the other end (Nationalists) entered into a direct armed conflict. Stalin felt compelled to support the Spanish Communist cause and sent a section of his Red Army to fight the fascist Nationalist Army.

Soon the 'Big Brother' attitude of the Soviet Union came to the fore as the Red Army demanded the rest of the Republican troops to subordinate to them for strategic purposes. The Spanish Republicans submitted reluctantly but the Russian Red Army committed numerous strategic errors resulting in a number of Republican deaths. Also the Red Army reporting directly to Stalin was always suspicious of POUM cadre for their Trotskyist leanings. Soon the tensions began to surface and the Republican camp was rent with virtual infighting.

This made the numerically inferior Nationalist camp more powerful than its Republican opponent and by the end of 1939, General Franco and his troops managed to defeat the Republicans. Franco immediately ordered the purging of thousands of Republican sympathisers in Spain, and the peninsula remained fascist till his death in 1975.

Aftermath of the Spanish Civil war:

The victory of the Republicans in the Spanish parliamentary elections in 1936 had given hopes to millions of people across Europe who were afraid of the impending Fascist danger. Hitler wanted to annexe the whole of Europe and hence supported General Franco's troops, in order to incorporate Spain into his Fascist bloc. The Republican side led by Communists generated great sympathy from all parts of the world including India which provided medical and financial aid under the supervision of Jawaharlal Nehru. Civilians from England, France and some communist countries joined the Republican cause and sacrificed their lives willingly. More importantly, Stalin's Russia helped in mobilising support for Spain from all over the world, as a result of which the USSR seized the moral higher ground for a while. The military assistance from USSR was immense and during the early days of the war, intellectuals began to take a very sympathetic view of Stalin.

Petty internal ideological clashes, overbearing attitude of Soviet soldiers towards their Spanish comrades, Stalin's apathy towards providing aid to Spain in the key phases of the war were some of the factors that led to the defeat of the Republican side. The Spanish debacle ended up severely damaging the morale of the International (Anti-Fascist) Resistance movement which soon were to face another blow in the form of the Ribbentrop-Molotov pact of 1939.

CHAPTER III

A Theoretical Detour

Before we get further into the narrative, a quick dive into what essentially is meant by Capitalism, Marxism and Fascism will help us understand the ideological undercurrents that drove the turbulent events of the Second World War (1939-1945).

Capitalism - Origins:

The period of 'Enlightenment' in Europe is broadly assumed to begin from the French revolution of 1779. The French revolution marked the defeat of the feudal classes and the nobility at the hands of the mercantile and the working classes. As a result, the mercantile classes (who dominated international trade) being the wealthier among the two, naturally assumed political and economic hegemony over that of the other, throughout Europe (the French Revolution triggered similar crises in the rest of European countries and ensured the disenfranchisement of clergy-nobility-feudal conglomerate in favour of the mercantile classes).

The mercantile classes soon grew up to become Industrial capitalists with the advent of the Great Industrial Revolution of the late 1700s. Mechanised production of commodities broke hitherto existing social bonds and created newer forms of association among the masses. Feudal agriculture rapidly gave way to modern industries and huge masses of peasants had to adapt to the changing needs of the newly created 'market'. Farmers, artisans, priests and the like lost their traditional bondage to their respective occupations to congeal into one homogenous whole called as the 'Industrial Proletariat'. In a few decades, this restructuring of societal and economic relations began to have telling effects on the psyche of the average European.

The new-born European worker now felt one with a lot of other industrial workers like him and his narrow, primitive identities were rapidly disappearing. He soon realised that he was more overworked than before and the benefits of his hard work, he found out much to his alarm, were being shared more unequally than before. Also his knowledge of traditional crafts like pottery, weaving, dyeing, etc were no longer relevant, as machines and drills produced more goods with much less effort and time. In huge factories where the division of labour was at the highest, all his work was restricted to accessory and supervisory duties. This soon led to a terrible alienation between himself and his output since he had only a very minimal role in producing it. Extreme division of labour led to massive labour deskilling while a highly skewed distribution of created wealth started generating extreme income inequalities. The political consequences of these sudden and unforeseen changes were also equally significant. Marxist ideas spread all over Europe which stressed the need for integration of the working classes transcending national and racial barriers. Trade Unions were forged based on the new found 'proletarian unity' whose potential for collective bargaining served as a counterweight to the ruling/exploiting classes. In many ways by late 1800s, Britain, France, Germany and other industrialised European nations witnessed the ossification of different races, tribes and communities of people into two broad approximate classes- the capitalist and the proletariat (working classes). This phase of socio-economic evolution was, in Marxist terms, called the Capitalist phase.

What was good in Capitalism?

The improvements achieved in intercontinental seafaring, the invention of the steam engine coupled with rapid spread of 'Enlightenment' values like secularism, freedom of expression, adult franchise, scientific outlook and human equality liberated European masses from their centuries-old feudal chains and pushed them into the Age of Industrial Capitalism. For the first time in human history, millions of people from different geographical locations and diverse backgrounds started working under one roof for a single capitalist. Commodity production during the previous era was petty, in the sense that a weaver in the town of Leicester, on nine out of ten occasions, made cloth for a carpenter who lived only a few miles away from his house. The demand hence, was mostly local and production, therefore was only limited whereas under Capitalism, demand was less local than otherwise and as a result, production was inevitably large-scale. To meet both internal and external demand for industrial commodities, agriculture was unofficially discouraged and a peasant uprooted from a town like Yorkshire was forced to rub shoulders with another peasant from Manchester whilst waiting in the long, serpentine queue to get his daily wage from his new factory employer. Races, cultures, languages and religions dissolved quickly into the melting pot of urban civilisation which marked the beginning of a new chapter in the process of social evolution.

The exchange of different ideas along with the growing popularity of path-breaking scientific theories (Darwin's theory of natural selection played a huge role) forced common men to revisit their adherences to traditional religious belief systems. The ability of science to analyse, explain and predict natural phenomena soon began to break the hegemony of local clergymen. Defiance of bishops and priests by the common people soon meant defiance of nobility and serfdom. In most of the countries, lands were owned by Churches and nobles whose methods of exploitation of the peasantry were heavily dependent on carefully preserved superstitious beliefs. Archbishops and godmen made local laws without a semblance of democracy, in close nexus with the nobles and the royal administrators. The transition to industrial Capitalism, therefore meant the overpowering and marginalisation of completely unscientific and obsolescent relations of production which left the disenfranchised ruling classes biding their time for revenge.

What makes Capitalism dig its own grave?

"What the bourgeoisie, therefore, produces, above all, is its own grave-diggers. Its fall and the victory of the proletariat are equally inevitable"

This was Karl Marx in the late 1800s when Industrial Europe was waking up to the unforeseen, yet dramatic effects of the new capitalist relations of production.

Let us first look at why Capitalism is often equated with 'exploitation' by Marxist writers. Capitalism, according to Marx survives on the most important condition of 'accumulation of surplus value'. Surplus value here refers to the amount of labour that a worker offers to the capitalist, more than what he is paid for*. Under Capitalism, on every single day, a worker is forced to sell his labour for a price that equals only the cost of replenishing his laboring potential for yet another day of work. But the commodity he produces and hands over to the capitalist has a 'market' value which is almost twice than what he is being paid**.

This extraction of surplus labour power out of the worker helps the capitalist to acquire a disproportionately larger share of created wealth. Hence this system of production relations breeds economic inequality leading to an ever widening chasm between the rich and the poor.

With the advancement in technology, capitalists find it easier to replace labour with machinery and this in turn creates a permanent industrial reserve army of unemployed people. The more the capitalist accumulates, the more his tendency to mechanise production and the more mechanised an industry gets, more number of people find themselves scrambling for a rapidly shrinking number of jobs. Hence the presence of an industrial reserve army helps the capitalist to keep wages low and extract more labour.

During the beginning of the capitalist cycle when the supply is suitably met by commensurate demand, the economy is alive and kicking as the domestic consumption is higher and the growing demand for goods, in turn creates more and more jobs (Boom). More jobs means more money at the hands of the workers to spend and hence the cycle continues efficiently. Competition among businesses tends to reduce market prices and a concomitant overproduction of goods triggers deflation and a further downward spiral of prices. To compensate for the falling prices which means a lower rate of profit, the capitalist resorts to replacing labour with machinery. But soon at a particular juncture, the unsustainability of the cycle comes to the surface when all the competing capitalists resort to mechanisation of production triggering a wave of worker retrenchment. When more workers find themselves out of jobs, their consumption reduces which in turn reduces domestic demand. Lesser demand can be met with lesser labour and lesser machinery and this throws another round of workers out of the workforce. This cycle builds and builds and all we have at the end is a terrible phase of stagnation and ubiquitous poverty (Bust).

During these phases of bust, the workers find themselves at sea and look for political solutions for their economic problems. The feudal era didn't produce much goods and hence barely offered any scope for massive unilateral accumulation by one particular class. The feudalist system mandated a particular share of the agricultural produce to be handed over by the tiller to the landlord and allowed him to keep the rest for himself. Artisans and craftsmen worked in collaborative formations called guilds which involved communities of people taking care of both production and marketing themselves. The created value, hence was being distributed more or less equally among themselves and the scope for exploitation was quite minimal. Most importantly, the feudal era witnessed very less unemployment even though poverty was widely prevalent.

But for the first time in history under capitalism, the human society found itself not only tremendously unequal but also, in contrast, unmistakably pregnant with a new and a radical idea seeded by the finest values of European Enlightenment and nourished by the ruthless excesses of capitalist exploitation, whose time for emergence, it was widely believed, had fortunately come.

Why Marxism?

Falling wages and rising unemployment, compulsory overtime for workers, labour deskilling and worker 'alienation', widespread poverty and growing starvation, ever increasing income inequalities, all of which together tended to drive the average European to extreme desperation. He was terribly confused as to why he couldn't buy enough bread even when there was a glut in the market. He couldn't understand why all of a sudden the knowledge of his inherited occupation was deemed completely useless. He couldn't understand how marbled palatial houses and luxury restaurants sprang beside cesspools dotted with nasty shacks and soot-covered huts. He couldn't understand why an unemployed adult was respected less than a child- labourer inside a family. He couldn't understand why more and more people were beginning to resort to any means at hand, to extract an extra cent from the other.

The publishing of Das Kapital in 1867 by Karl Marx took a long while to trigger tsunamis that it was meant to, in political and intellectual circles. Marx wrote another masterpiece which went by the name 'The Communist Manifesto' in collaboration with his friend Friedrich Engels. These seminal books along with a few more came to form the theoretical basis of Marxian Socialism.

Marx was the first popular intellectual in Europe to analyse, contextualise and predict the future progress of Industrial Capitalism thereby answering almost all the questions of the confused average European. The Communist Manifesto envisioned a Utopian society of the future that would exist without a government where people did occupations that they were naturally good at and earned enough to satisfy their daily basic needs. People shared all work with each other in small agglomerations called Communes where social, racial and economic hierarchies had no business to exist. The lack of a government meant complete absence of a police force since it was believed that a Communist society would have no exploitation and hence no scope for crime. People were to be judged based on what they actually capable of rather than by the amount of economic value they created. In other words, Communism called for the complete obliteration of traditionally oppressive, social, racial and economic structures and invited every worker, peasant and craftsman in every country to dissolve himself in the great international proletarian sea.

As you may see, Communist ideas had plenty of reasons to appeal to large masses of people across countries and continents beckoning all of them to join in the revolutionary struggle against the exploiting propertied classes. Marxism, in other words called for a scientific, rational and egalitarian society which spelt nothing less than a formidable threat to the existence of all currently hegemonic classes that have been thriving hitherto purely based on exploitation.

Why Fascism?

To accurately define the ideological contours of fascism is a completely useless task since fascism is anything but ideological. Fascism can suitably be reduced to a logical approximation of many-hued yet uniformly impulsive calls for self-defence by all the existing or rapidly dwindling hegemonic classes in response to the inescapable threat from the disgruntled proletariat.

Any country under consideration, it is to be noted, does not move seamlessly from one form of production relations into another as a whole, in one single stroke. Feudal or semi feudal forms may co-exist for a while with advanced capitalist forms until the latter consumes the former completely. As a result, these feudal classes do continue to exist, exerting their influence on national politics as well even if their presence is rudimentary. In various countries, these feudal classes form the backbone of right wing fascist movements reminding people of their pre-capitalist identities such as race, religion and communities. Their influence on public opinion is never to be underestimated because identity politics comes in handy even for their capitalist allies in order to break the unity of the rising proletariat.

When the masses are confused as to why they remain poor and deprived of opportunities even when national wealth as a whole is increasing, only Marxism responds to them accurately by pointing fingers at the exploiting propertied classes. Solely to counter this challenge, Fascism looms up to instantly divert the attention of the masses away from the propertied classes towards the masses themselves, blaming everything on a tiny racial or religious or a national minority with a view to breaking their new-found proletarian unity. This can be understood better if we relate this phenomenon to that occurring in India under the current Hindu Nationalist regime where the establishment keeps blaming Muslims and Pakistanis whenever uncomfortable questions regarding economy are raised.

Fascism, in addition to attacking Marxism does not shy away from targeting the values of 'Enlightenment' as well- secularism, liberalism, scientific outlook, democracy and free speech, etc. solely because these ideals were instrumental in the construction of the Marxist theory. In short, Fascism is against anything that is deemed progressive, and hence often referred in common parlance as wholly 'reactionary' in nature.

Now that we are sufficiently abreast of the ideological basis of early 20th century European crisis, we can comfortably return to our story.

Economic Depression of 1929 and rise of Fascism:

By the end of the 1920s, the industrial United States and Western Europe had exhausted the 'boom' phase of their capitalist cycle and were fast dwindling into the inevitable phase of 'bust'. 1929 was the year when an unprecedented Stock Market crash occurred in the US which triggered a cascading economic collapse in all countries commercially linked to the economic superpower. Italy, France, Germany, Britain and other trading partners of US were the worst hit with millions of workers losing jobs everyday thereby setting off a crisis in almost all sectors of their national economies.

The Russian Revolution which had installed a Communist Government at the helm of the largest country in the world, had been inspiring Communist movements in almost all parts of the world ever since 1917. Since the end of the First World War, Germany was showing all signs of suitably following the Russian model when the electoral influence of the German Communist Party was growing manifold. In parallel, special circumstances such as the imposition of the humiliating Versailles treaty on Germany by all the other Western powers at the end of the WW1 and the dismantling of the Second Reich at the same time to pave way for democracy, also had given necessary and sufficient grounds for the revival of German nationalism.

The interaction of Communist and the contrarian Nationalist influences on the psyche of the average German produced remarkable societal effects. The economic depression whose impacts were manifest in the early 1930s squelched all public confidence in the parliamentary system of democracy and drove Germans to find solutions in authoritarian models. Strategic blunders time and again by the German Communist party along with the reluctance of the centre-left Social Democrats to sufficiently diagnose the extent of the Fascist pestilence led to the electoral victory of Adolf Hitler's National Socialist Party (Nazi) in 1933. The Nazi party grew on inherent, yet rudimentary anti-semitism of the Germans and amplified it disproportionately to suit its political ends. The economic troubles of the country were blamed on both the Jews and the Western Powers and Hitler called for ostracization of the local Jews to ensure Aryan racial purity. German Fascism inspired similar movements in Poland, Austria and even in the United States.

Keep your friends close, enemies closer:

Hitler assumed power in 1933 and soon passed a series of acts that were aimed at undermining democratic institutions. The Communist party was banned and a great purge of Communist and trade union leaders followed. Jews were handpicked from every nook and corner of the country's streets and forced to work in ghettos (concentration camps). Hitler abolished the post of the President with the death of Hindenburg and declared himself, the sole Chancellor of Germany. He called his new Government 'the Third Reich', a reference to Germany's supposedly glorious years under monarchy.

The rise of Hitler alarmed communists all over the world and his alliance with Italian Fascist dictator Benito Mussolini raised a lot of eyebrows in the Western Capitalist camp as well. Hitler kept bullying his smaller sovereign neighbours with Nazi military might and kept on signing a string of treaties allowing German expansion into the West. Most of these treaties were blessed by the reluctance of French, British and American Governments to confront Hitler since none of these countries were by the end of the 1930s ready to venture into another war. Russia's Stalin continued to call for strategic alliances with the Western

Powers to counter the threat of Hitler and kept his propaganda machinery working overtime to keep people all over the world ever vigilant to the rising threat of Fascism. Communist parties all over the world were ordered by Stalin to take the lead in countering local fascist movements. When none of the Western Powers responded positively to his calls, Stalin was forced to fend for himself at the end.

Hitler by the end of 1938 had managed to re-arm Germany to its pre-1914 strength. Millions of marks were spent on arms and ammunition manufacturing while the size of the German armed forces grew manifold during the Nazi years. Hitler was now setting his sights far higher. He wanted to bring the whole of Europe under his control but was equally wary of the threat posed by his Communist neighbour. He wasn't ready at that point of time to open a war at two fronts simultaneously and hence decided to reserve Russia for the future.

So he called for a non-aggression agreement with Russia to which a desperate Stalin acquiesced immediately, culminating in the Molotov- Ribbentrop pact signed on August 23, 1939 at Moscow. The pact recognised mutual sovereignty and mandated non-interference into each other's expansionist aims. In addition, Germany and Russia recognised mutual 'spheres of influence' in Europe in the future event of a possible rearrangement of territories belonging to Poland and the Baltic countries. Hitler's hand was enormously strengthened by this historic pact with Stalin which propelled him to attack Poland the very next week on September 1, 1939, that unforgettable date often considered to be the date of the beginning of the Second World War.

Stalin, on the other hand knew very well that the only tangible advantage that the pact had given him was nothing more than an interim breathing space that could enable him to plan for the gruesome inevitable - that final face-off against the formidable Germany, which was expected to happen sooner than later, even if Hitler was proving to be unusually amiable to him, for the time being.

*a very difficult attempt has been made by me to simplify Marxist theory of surplus value as much as possible. I hereby acknowledge the possible inaccuracy of my assertion with respect to what Marx had actually said.

**the prices and values were calculated by Marx in Capital Volume 1 based on hypothetical market conditions.

CHAPTER IV

Blood, Blood Everywhere

Josef Stalin, when he assumed the mantle in 1922 was initially considered to be a worthy successor to the legacy of the founder-leader Vladimir Lenin by the masses. Stalin worked hard to build on that image and tried to establish a cult of personality everywhere in and around Russia. State media were ordered to sing 'paeans' to Stalin and his persona while it was also true that the masses did buy that 'image' obediently. Communist parties of other countries, affiliated to the Communist International were also forced to bow before Stalin's supremacy and dissidents if any, were expelled even if their sincerity to the movement was beyond doubt.

But Stalin, just like any other dictator had plenty of insecurities. Having undergone the rigmaroles of intra-party power struggles himself, Stalin was uncomfortable at the thought of having to encounter political manipulators (like him) and other popular revolutionaries who may, at an unexpected point of time, given the lack of proper intra party democracy, stake their claim to leadership. Also, Stalin's obsession with immediate results with respect to economy which might help validate his political superiority began to have totally unforeseen and sickening consequences.

When Stalin ordered forced collectivisation of agriculture, peasants who received land during Lenin's NEP started rebelling. Rebellions spread throughout Russia which only ended up evoking even more repressive measures from the State. Soon, thousands of farmers were sent to Siberian concentration camps where they were left to toil all day and freeze to death. Within a couple of years, the consequences of forced collectivisation were felt all over the country with thousands dying from food shortages and inhuman working conditions.

The ruling Communist Party which still had a healthy number of selfless and devoted founder-members in its ranks, was beginning to crack apart. Stalin's policies came up for discussion during party meetings and scathing accusations were hurled up against him by party factions led by Leon Trotsky. Nikolai Bukharin, another popular founder-member now in Stalin's camp was soon to join the opposition. With a large number of popular leaders rallying against Stalin, what he did next to retain power, was virtually unparalleled in its brutality and scale, by any other event in human history so far.

Gliding over all:

1933 was the year when Stalin's aide Sergei Kirov was mysteriously assassinated. This was followed by a series of executions of all popular leaders who refused to toe the line of Stalin. Thousands of party leaders, workers and intellectuals who had given up all their personal ambitions for witnessing the creation of Communist Russia during their lifetime were officially declared 'counter-revolutionaries' and hence executed immediately.

Soon the purge extended into other domains as well - scientists, artists, teachers, military personnel, union leaders, bureaucrats, engineers who were suspected of anti-Stalinism were found and weeded out. Even people who had been previously associated with Trotsky but had later switched camps were not excluded. A work of art which had no reference to the 'glory of the Revolution', a valid scientific argument that ran counter to the government's policy, an article in the newspaper that sounded like admiring the West were enough and sufficient evidences as to warrant trial and persecution. Most of the Communist leaders were subjected to physical and mental torture and were forced to sign 'voluntary' confessions of having indulged in 'acts of treason and sabotage'. Eric Hobsbawm, a left wing British historian in one of his essays mentions that due to both man-made starvation and Stalin's purges, the annual growth rate of the entire Soviet Population itself fell drastically during the 1930s and took some years to rebound.

Leon Trotsky who managed to escape Soviet Russia, after a number of years of active political life in the West was assassinated in Mexico in 1940. By the end of 1938, the Communist Party had been wiped clean of Stalin's detractors and even of those few who had some independent line of reasoning. Stalin brought some more amendments to the Soviet constitution so as to make him the most powerful leader in the whole of the Union. Vesting almost all decision making powers into the position of the General Secretary of the Party would have telling consequences in the future including that of the downfall of the Soviet Union itself.

Stalin joins Hitler's party:

Hitler attacked Poland on September 1, 1939 which invited both England and France into the World War. Poland fell within a few weeks and the Soviet Union was invited to share the spoils. Baltic countries such as Latvia, Estonia and Lithuania were also soon annexed by Soviet forces aided by the Nazi troops. Soon the Soviet Union and the Nazis signed a bilateral trade agreement which promised mutual exchange of food, consumer durables and military equipment during the course of the war.

The Russo- Nazi joint action in Europe was a terrible embarrassment for Communist parties world over which had been so far, steadfast and single-minded in their opposition to Fascism. However, the parties were not ready to alienate Soviet help for their local activities and hence decided to toe Stalin's line dutifully. A large number of influential economists and intellectuals all over Europe quit the Communist party during this time as more atrocities were about to follow. The KGB officials handed a lot of German communists who were hitherto given political asylum in the USSR to the German State Police in adherence to certain secret statutes in the Ribbentrop-Molotov pact.

By 1940, Germany and USSR had grown so close to each other that the former invited the latter to join the Axis Powers and fight the West as a single cohesive bloc. But the Soviet Union was, in parallel on a rampage over its erstwhile territories (of the Tsarist era) annexing Finland and marauding Romania all of which mildly disturbed Hitler. Also there were several disagreements over demarcation in the captured territories between the Nazi and Red Army chiefs which, however were mutually agreed to be put to rest for the time being.

The beginning of the end of Adolf Hitler:

Hitler right from his days as a street politician harbored a grudge towards Communists and the Slavs. In his autobiography Mein Kampf, he had written about his dreams of bringing the whole of Russia under Aryan rule. As soon as he assumed power, his first target was the Communists followed by the Jews and other 'inferior' races like the Slavs. Even if Hitler busied himself with efforts to pay Britain and France in the same coin for their collusive efforts in humiliating Germany through the Versailles,

Soviet Russia was always at the back of his mind.

But nothing emboldened him to attack Russia in 1941 itself as much as his massive military victories over Poland, Denmark, Belgium, Norway and Luxembourg. Most importantly, Hitler was overjoyed when Nazi troops along with those of Italy, conquered France within just 46 days of combat. By December 1940, just within less than one and half years of the start of the Great War, Germany had managed to bring more than half of Western Europe under its thumb.

Hitler's prestige soared all over Nazi Germany and he was considered the true successor to the glorious legacy of the erstwhile Reich Empire. Till 1940, Hitler had defied a lot of advice given by his military generals and easy, continuous victories did a great deal to bolster his confidence. His complacency was soon on display in the beginning of 1941 when he was poring over Germany's plans to attack the Soviet Union. Hitler was right in assuming that Stalin had purged a majority of his top military personnel in the 1930s itself and hence had to rely on inexperienced officials in the event of a war. Hitler also looked at the very slow progress made by the Red Army against the supposedly weak Finns during the Winter War of 1939-40 and felt that he could safely rely on the ineptitude of the Soviet military machine in his plans to advance his attack on the Soviet Union, at least by a year.

Hitler also believed that the Russian citizens were terribly oppressed by Stalin and his pliant bureaucracy and hence a German invasion would possibly be welcomed by them as a means towards their liberation. He is supposed to have remarked to his colleagues, 'We will just kick the door of the house and I am sure the whole structure will come down!'

Stalin on the other hand, ignored warnings emanating from Britain and his own secret service about an impending Nazi invasion in mid-1941 and strongly believed that Hitler would not be ready to open a war on two fronts simultaneously. Hitler meanwhile was mobilising his troops for a war against Russia which he wanted to be unprecedentedly barbaric in its ruthlessness, violating all codes of warfare. Just like how the Nazis had exterminated more than a million Poles as soon as they occupied Poland, the Wehrmacht (Unified armed forces of Germany) were instructed to be equally brutal on Russian civilians and to loot all their material possessions in order to support further Nazi advance.

Hitler coined a new name for his campaign against Russia, ignoring crucial warnings by his generals on climate and logistics and launched Operation Barbarossa on June 22, 1941.

CHAPTER V

The Wall

Inspite of forced collectivisation of agriculture and consequent mass discontent over Stalin's policies, the over emphasis on industrialisation was beginning to produce considerable economic growth in the USSR. When the Industrial West was reeling under the after effects of economic depression, the USSR inspite of officially inflated figures, was considered a growing economy by various economists. Economic planning by the Centre which was antithetical to the capitalist mode of production was now viewed favorably by the capitalist countries affected by the Depression. Soviet Industrial output was hugely dependent on the military requirements of Russia guided by Stalin's impressive foresight. Though there were failed industrial experiments here and there, the Soviet Economy managed to compensate by increasing the working hours of the industrial laborers substantially.

The USSR by the end of 1930s, had a better industrial economy, exponentially greater military strength both in terms of men and munition, a more disciplined bureaucracy and a greater mass of regimented party cadre than it had during the previous tumultuous decade. These were aspects that Hitler might have failed to countenance during the drafting of the plans for Operation Barbarossa.

Ever since the conclusion of the Ribbentrop-Molotov pact in 1939, the USSR media found it expedient to tone down anti-Fascist propaganda in order not to provoke Hitler. Even by early 1941, when signs of Nazi hostility were beginning to surface, Stalin could not bring himself to consider the possibilities of a Nazi invasion the same year, unless an overt provocation was made from their end. However this was exactly what Hitler had badly needed - a surprise attack that would stun Stalin into abject submission.

First Blood:

Hitler overwhelmed by victories over Western Europe was buoyant when Britain started showing signs of breaking under unrelenting air attacks by the German Luftwaffe. And Operation Barbarossa, he presumed would end within a couple of months with Stalin surrendering to the totally unforeseen Nazi mobilization.

The operation which began in June 1941 was multi-pronged with fronts being opened on all sides of the world's largest country with an unbending intent to decimate the Russians. Soviet resistance was obviously weak and they lost control of Northern Finland, Ukraine, Belarus by September 1941. Hitler was happy to have taken the city of Smolensk which had a direct 400 km road to Moscow and the Nazi press was jubilant to inform the German masses that they were just a few weeks away from a historic victory over Russia.

But Nazi soldiers, contrary to their expectations realised soon that the Russian civilians were not ready to betray their country so easily. In fact, to their shock, the Nazis could see a vast number of civilians actively enlisting in the Red Army with great patriotism especially when Leningrad came under siege. The peasants before fleeing their villages made sure that their crops were burned, cattle killed and possessions destroyed in order to deprive the invaders of necessary supplies. Hitler's move to launch Barbarossa earlier than planned was heavily dependent on the possibility of seizure of Russian resources for Nazi military purposes but the Scorched Earth policy of the Russians was completely unexpected. Their move to take Ukraine's capital Kiev which was full of oil resources took a great toll on their army strength even though they succeeded in their mission eventually.

By October 1941, Hitler was getting reports of victories on all fronts in USSR even though complaints of supply inadequacies were slowly cropping up. He now pressed his men forward to take Moscow next which, as we shall see was a terrible strategic error, for it was precisely the time when winter was setting quickly all over Western Russia.

Red Heat:

The Nazis were just less than 150 km away from Moscow when snow and rains began to damage road lines leading to the capital city. German tanks were not used to such terrain despite which by November 1941, the Nazi soldiers were able to confidently report to Berlin that they could smell Kremlin just a few miles away. But the Russian winter intensified with sudden blizzards tearing the terrain to shreds. This in turn rendered air attacks totally impossible and hence German supplies were terribly hit. The Nazis had no other choice but to wait for a couple of weeks to carry out any further advance. Stalin on the other hand immediately summoned the forces on the Siberian front (guarding the Russo-Japanese borders) and mobilised plenty of divisions to defend the capital city. Russian soldiers naturally had no issues fighting amid the relentless winter and their tanks were better engineered to negotiate unreliable terrain. The Soviet fightback near Moscow was magnificent and the Nazis were successfully expelled out of Moscow's vicinity in a month-long counter offensive. By January 1942, Hitler had to acknowledge secretly that the Battle of Moscow was a debacle and that without a revision of strategy, there would be even more reversals. Meanwhile Stalin felt that it was his chance to take Hitler by surprise and ordered the launching of counter offensives in all German occupied territories. He substantially increased outlays for armament and aircraft production. Nazis' subsequent attempts to capture Azerbaijan were also severely thwarted by the Red Army and the intensifying winter. Germany also found itself severely lacking in oil in order to meet its increasing fuel demands.

By mid-1942 itself, the Russians had, owing to initial reversals lost close to a million soldiers and infrastructure worth billions. But Stalin's dynamic leadership ensured that the morale of the Red Army and the civilian populace never plummeted as a result of which their soldiers fought difficult battles more valiantly than their German counterparts.

Saviour Stalin:

Two battles that occurred in the next two years decisively changed the course of the war- the Battle of Stalingrad (October 1942 - February 1943) and the Battle of Kursk (July to August 1943). Hitler after facing reversals at Moscow now shifted his sights onto the industrial town called Stalingrad which served as one of the biggest manufacturing hubs in the Soviet Union. The capture of Stalingrad and destruction of the city, Hitler believed shall choke the Soviet war Economy completely. Nazis also wanted to seize the water routes of Volga River which could easily be facilitated by the capture of Stalingrad. The water routes could help Germans to manage supply lines and also aid them in their march towards oil-rich Baku.

The battle for Stalingrad took place for over six months with Nazis achieving key breakthroughs initially. In fact in the first four months, the Germans captured more than ninety percent of the town's area and went on to destroy factories. The civilian population was not evacuated properly by the Red Army which led to a lot of casualties. However the Red Army soldiers fought from unconventional positions in the city such as the sewers, rooms in evacuated office buildings posing stiff resistance. Soon the Nazis were flabbergasted to see a few divisions of the Russian army consisting of women soldiers and even untrained civilians. Towards January 1943, the Sixth Army of the Germans was surrounded on all sides by newer divisions of the Red Army and all supply lines from Germany were successfully cut off. Close to 200,000 soldiers were locked inside the town and they had to depend solely on the supplies from the Luftwaffe. As weeks passed, the visiting Luftwaffe planes were attacked by those of the Soviet air force and the number of operative aircraft at the invader's side was fast dwindling. By February 1943, Hitler took over as the Chief Commander of the Wehrmacht and he vehemently rejected appeals from the Sixth Army to surrender at Stalingrad. Meanwhile, the armament factories located east of Urals in Russia were operating at full capacity and newer military equipment was supplied at a rapid pace to the Red Army. By the end of February, the famished and demoralised Sixth Army decided to surrender to the Russians infuriating an intransigent Hitler. The battle of Stalingrad is considered to be the bloodiest battle in human history with casualties on both sides amounting to millions. Victory in the battle of Kursk followed the same year for the Russians and by then, the Germans had virtually been pushed into the defensive.

Stalin was hailed all over the world for his effective leadership and the international press was forced to hail Russians for their wonderful resistance. Meanwhile, the tables had turned on in the West with Japan drawing a dormant United States into the war and Hitler had to oversee military operations on two fronts none of which were giving good news. Italy's surrender to the Allies in 1943 also struck a solid blow to the fortunes of Axis powers. Stalin ordered the Red Army to march into Germany following the liberation of the occupied territories. The Wehrmacht was by early 1945 draining the German economy while Hitler was fast losing his allies.

Observers in America including top military personnel admitted that Communist Russia almost single handedly managed to stop the inexorably perilous Nazi advance at a massive human and economic cost. Close to 25 million Russians had been killed during their struggle against the Nazis and the Soviet Economy slumped back into yet another crisis.

Adolf Hitler, having been surrounded by Allied troops on all sides, in May 1945 committed suicide at Berlin. The Nazi soldiers who had massacred millions of Jews, POWs in the occupied areas were punished at the Nuremberg trials.

Josef Stalin once decried by the world as a contemptible barbarian, had now established himself in the world scene as the Hero who saved the World from the jaws of Fascism. The stature of the USSR among the world powers was now completely undeniable and this led to the inclusion of the country in the new-born United Nations as one of its five Permanent members. But the completely unexpected emergence of USSR as the defender of world peace, sovereignty and equality had more lasting and dangerous repercussions. From 1945 onwards it would be in Berlin, the world's erstwhile fountainhead of Fascism that the edifice to mark newer and bigger ideological clashes of the future would be constructed, in the form of the Wall that divided the city into its Western and Eastern halves.

CHAPTER VI

The Swansong

The massive victory achieved by the USSR in the epochal Second World War had helped boost the prestige of the Union as well that of its ruler. The public mood, by and large was celebratory and the people were relieved that the three-year long war which had taken a devastating toll on their lives and possessions had finally ended. Russia was able to annex a lot of territories from various European countries and Stalin foisted Communist Governments in countries like Poland while he was happy to see a few like Yugoslavia and Czechoslovakia turning Communist out of their own volition. Yugoslavia had fought on the side of the Allies led by the valiant Joseph Broz Tito against the Axis Powers and immediately after the war the charismatic Marshal took over the reins of the country with widespread public support and limited Soviet help. The Baltic countries were also brought under Soviet influence and almost every ruling Communist Party had to report to Stalin on almost all key internal affairs.

Russians, for generations together are often believed to have preferred iron fisted rulers over soft ones and hence submission to Stalin's autocracy, according to a few historical accounts, was treated by the populace as a way of paying obeisance to their Holy Fatherland. When Russia was pulled into 'The Great Patriotic War' in 1942, Stalin's abrupt move to reinstate the legacies of some of Tsarist Russia's erstwhile rulers was met with rousing patriotism and great fervor among the masses. The State propaganda machines invoked the achievements of Peter the Great and other legendary Tsars and loud calls to restore the Great Russian Pride were issued relentlessly. Stalin also ensured that a broad base of public support was achieved at this time of crisis by promptly relaxing restrictions on free speech and the practice of religion. Thousands of prisoners were released from concentration camps and were expected to enlist in the army while Catholic Churches were summoned to align themselves with the State's war effort. Stalin's tactics at the time of national emergency, needless to say bore fruit and it is very much to the credit of the average Russian soldier that the looming Fascist pestilence was eradicated once and for all from the face of the Earth (except in Spain). People, in return naturally expected permanent withdrawal of repressive measures along with concrete steps by the State towards betterment of their living conditions. But what happened later was just quite the opposite.

Tito wags the middle finger:

Marshal Tito, right from the installation of the Communist Republic in Yugoslavia in 1945 was averse to the overbearing attitudes of Soviet Russia and was bent on taking an independent line. He also tried to split the Communist Bloc and form a separate federation in order to countervail excessive Russian interference. When civil war broke out in Greece in 1946, Tito much to the chagrin of the USSR sent troops of his own accord to aid the Grecian Communist camp while Stalin due to a compact with the Western Powers, had promised them neutrality prevailing over other East European republics to remain silent. Stalin had also planted informers inside the Yugoslavian Communist Party but Tito didn't think twice before finding and eliminating them. Tito even before his victorious military campaign against the Axis, had enjoyed great popularity among his countrymen and hence had very little necessity of Moscow's assistance to come to power.

Tito's insubordination to Stalin led to the expulsion of Yugoslavia from the Communist International (Comintern) in 1948 (until the rupture was healed in 1955 under a different Soviet leadership). However Stalin was worried too much about Tito setting 'an unhealthy precedent' for other satellite countries to follow, that he even made unsuccessful arrangements for an invasion of Yugoslavia by the end of the 1940s. Stalin's insecurity is apparent in one of the letters Tito wrote to the former, which goes as follows:

'Dear Stalin, stop sending your men to kill me. I have captured five of them. If I send one to kill you, there won't be need for a second'.

Russians return to 'normalcy':

The Russian citizens on the other hand were to witness something that they had least expected. Stalin shocked everyone by ordering demotion and transfer of successful war-time military heads of the Red Army to other less powerful positions and resumed the 'purges' for which he was so notorious for. Sizes of concentration camps were restored almost to their pre-war levels and civil rights were curbed once again. The masses were exhorted to work longer hours and factories were set impossible targets in order to resuscitate the war-ravaged economy.

Stalin, however, was slowly receding from the centre-stage owing to age related illnesses from the late 1940s and other leaders started helping him manage daily affairs. China meanwhile had succeeded in becoming Communist under the dynamic leadership of Mao Zedong with strong support from the Soviet Union. The People's Republic of China was established in 1949 and was expected to join the bandwagon of Soviet's satellites soon. However, Moscow was to realize shortly that Mao was not to be taken lightly.

With the Korean War drawing to a stalemate in 1953, Josef Stalin, a few months before the Korean armistice was signed, breathed his last on 5th March at the age of 74. Stalin was buried alongside founder patriarch Vladimir Lenin at the famous Lenin's Mausoleum on 9th March in the presence of leaders from various Soviet satellite states. Many countries condoled the passing away of the Soviet leader and India's Jawaharlal Nehru struck a sombre note in his speech to the Parliament, heaping accolades on one of the most paradoxical leaders of history.

'Anyhow a very great figure has passed away but Marshal Stalin was something much more than the head of a State. He was great in his own right way, whether he occupied the office or not'.

The third generation:

Josef Stalin, the Georgian revolutionary-turned dictator had no doubt, left the Soviet Union many times stronger and more influential in global affairs than it was before he took over. It is solely to the credit of that man, the son of a poor cobbler that the Union survived for as long as it did. But that doesn't explain everything about the position of Stalin in Russia's history. The rise of the USSR as a superpower at the end of the Second World War, though a phenomenal achievement given its horrible treatment at the hands of the Western powers in its formative years, was brought about at a humongous cost. Millions of workers were made to toil for more than twelve hours a day and thousands died due to overwork and terrible working conditions. Famines caused by forced collectivisation, outdated farming practices, distribution chain mismanagement and most importantly, willful neglect of public welfare killed close to 20 million people. Millions had to endure hellish conditions in concentration camps and not even half of those are estimated to have survived. Common citizens had to live their lives under constant surveillance perennially wary of the guillotine that dangled over their heads.

On the other hand, the Soviet bureaucracy while being servile and sycophantic to Stalin enjoyed numerous benefits and succeeded more often than not in getting around the law. Their tyranny on the common people was unchallenged as long as they dutifully toed the party line. Even when Stalin was informed about the excesses of the bureaucracy, there seems to be no record of any punitive orders issued from the top.

The party which initially grew on Marxist theories during the Tsar era had a lot of intellectuals in its ranks whose influence never allowed concentration of party power in a few hands. But ever since Lenin took over Russia, the party gradually started losing its democratic character at the altar of discipline and patriotism. With the ascent of Stalin, Lenin's 'democratic centralism' which emphasised the superior character of the party leadership (Politburo) over others, was to be rigorously applied. As the years passed, even the Politburo lost its decision making powers and handed its keys to the General Secretary of the CPSU once and for all. Lack of checks and balances in administration naturally led to rash and adventurous decision making and when the results turned out to be disastrous, the State immediately made quixotic U-turns committing even more blunders during its retreat. Stalin justified his wrongs whenever they were out in the open, as 'necessary destruction' that would only help the country's progress in the long run. If Fascism emphasized racial superiority to justify brutalities such as ethnic cleansing, Stalinism bred on its own groundless myths of infallibility to rationalise wanton violence and willful man-slaughter. As Communism spread across the world in the second half of the 20th century, Stalinism would find its devilish alter-egos in poorer countries such as China, Cambodia, etc. But the Communist Party of the Soviet Union, after the demise of Stalin did not continue to be intransigent and arrogant as was expected.

In 1956, at a time when the rest of the World had yet no inkling of what was transpiring in the USSR, a 60 year-old former military chief at the 20th Party Congress in Moscow, would stun the world with a shattering revelation:

'Stalin acted not through persuasion, explanation and patient cooperation with people, but by imposing his concepts and demanding absolute submission to his opinion. Whoever opposed these concepts or tried to prove his [own] viewpoint and the correctness of his [own] position was doomed to removal from the leadership collective and to subsequent moral and physical annihilation. This was especially true during the period following the 17th Party Congress, when many prominent Party leaders and rank-and-file Party workers, honest and dedicated to the cause of Communism, fell victim to Stalin's despotism'.

The speech titled 'On the Cult of Personality and its Consequences' delivered by the First Secretary of the CPSU, the de-facto leader of the USSR would mark a new departure in the history of the Empire. Nikita Khrushchev, a veteran who had led the famous defense of Stalingrad during the Great Patriotic War had ascended to the top seven months after Stalin's demise. Khrushchev, in retrospect, appears to be the first leader of the USSR who had more scruples than arrogance, more sincerity than dogmatism and most important of all, a genuine willingness to admit failure and learn from mistakes. That singular attitude, prompted him to deliver that epoch-making address that unravelled his predecessor publicly to the world, and bore testimony to his commitment to righteousness unmindful of the perilous consequences that were soon to follow.

THE HEYDAYS

CHAPTER VII

Half Human, Half Beast

Nikita Khrushchev was the son of a poor peasant. He was not highly educated but was well known for his organising skills. His military achievements had endeared him to Stalin and his proximity to the Dictator was envied by a lot of his colleagues namely Malenkov, Beria, etc. Khrushchev, it cannot be denied that he was party to Stalin's ruthless crimes during the Great Purges and was instrumental in implementing many of his orders obediently. He had become Stalin's trustworthy lieutenant after a point and had begun to exert his influence on national policy-making as well. Stalin, by early 1950s was fast growing senile and Khrushchev's radical ideas to revive Soviet agriculture interested him a lot. Khrushchev was allowed by Stalin to perform an experiment in some of Ukraine's villages called the 'The Agrotown Project' which

involved merging of smaller collectives into larger ones for better resource utilisation and increased productivity. The experiment failed badly and ended up handy for Khrushchev's rivals to undermine him in the upcoming power struggle. As Stalin's demise was becoming imminent, Malenkov with Beria were busy scouting for loyal recruits within the party who could be trusted to vote for their camp against that of Khrushchev.

Exorcising Stalin:

Khrushchev on the other hand kept pace with his rivals travelling around the country extensively delivering speeches exhorting masses to focus on agriculture. He, within just six months after Stalin's death had managed to gather great support from all over the country. His ambitious project named Virgin Lands involved bringing thousands of acres of land in Kazakhstan under cultivation to meet growing demand for food. Even though there were plenty of errors in the implementation of the project, results were turning out to be impressive. The supply of grains had grown as expected and Khrushchev's prestige rose within the ranks of the party. Meanwhile, Malenkov having succeeded Stalin immediately after his death as the First Secretary of the CPSU, had different long term plans. He badly wanted the party to exit

immediately from the ministries governing various branches of administration. He had plans to pull established technocrats and engineers into positions of authority so as to obliterate red-tapism and revive the vitals of the rusted administrative machinery. However this was not an adept move considering his tenuous position within the party. The top brass of the CPSU was obviously not willing to liberate the administration from its long tentacles and hence decided to side with Khrushchev. His flashy success at Virgin Lands embarrassed Malenkov terribly and by September 1953, Khrushchev was voted to become the First Secretary of the CPSU forcing the hapless Malenkov to resign.

Malenkov however continued to hold the position of Premier with Khrushchev remaining the Head of the State. Even though the two were bitter rivals, they both weren't ready to repeat Stalin's mistakes. They were unanimous in what was called Destalinisation which involved acquittal of millions of prisoners from concentration camps and rehabilitation of disgraced erstwhile party leaders. The press was considerably freed up while writers and intellectuals were allowed to voice their independent opinions. Even though its limits were strictly circumscribed, criticism of the government, it could safely be said that, was allowed for the first time in the history of the USSR only after the emergence of Khrushchev.

Officials could now indulge in discussions related to policy-making without the fear of being punished for speaking out candidly. Khrushchev by 1954, in a landmark move, had decided to decentralise powers vested in the Central Presidium allowing town councils and local authorities substantial latitude in managing administrative affairs. Independent farming was also encouraged by the State to stimulate production while procurement prices of grains were hiked considerably. Taxes were reduced and measures to mitigate shortage of consumer goods were implemented. The USSR in short, within a couple of years after Stalin's death slowly began to breathe freely.

A reformer's travails:

Khrushchev within a few years had made tremendous progress within the party outwitting rivals and consolidating his position to the extent of even forcing Premier Malenkov to resign (1956). Khrushchev's move to mobilise the satellite nations of the USSR under the Warsaw Pact as a counter offensive to America's NATO was a politically wise move as it reinforced the continuance of a global bipolarity on the imagination of millions of colonised people who were reeling under the yoke of Western Imperialism. Khrushchev's ambitious Housing Programme which allowed numerous citizens to gain private houses also enhanced his reputation further. On February 25 1956, at the 20th Party Congress, Khrushchev's shocking revelation of the excesses committed during Stalin's time, was a heroic gesture which won wholehearted praise from various parts of the world. However, it would be totally wrong to assume that Khrushchev had a smooth sailing throughout during his early years at the helm.

Khrushchev's shocking denunciation of Stalin created great unrest among the allies of the USSR as it ended up being an open repudiation of Moscow's own supposed infallibility. It must be remembered that the unity of the Eastern Bloc was built largely on Kremlin's supremacy and preservation of the same mandated extraordinary levels of vigilance on the part of the CPSU. It is reported that on the eve of the Party Congress, most of his colleagues were either totally unaware of Khrushchev's plans to denounce Stalin or were openly hostile to such ideas desperately advising him all the time to drop them. It is believed that Khrushchev's actions this time was dictated by a strong impulse of honesty surfacing out of a rankling conscience that forced him to shun political expediency in favour of an indirect confession of wrongdoing.

China was the first country to openly express dissatisfaction with Moscow's revelation and Mao, just like many other communist leaders started labelling Khrushchev as 'revisionist and counter-revolutionary'. Albania broke out of the Cominform the same year while dissidents in Hungary and Poland felt emboldened by Khrushchev's act. In a few months, Hungary tried to break out of the Soviet sphere of influence but Khrushchev sent his troops to crush the rebellion as brutally as possible. Khrushchev's rule till 1964, as we shall see would be characterized by similarly alternating displays of benevolence and cruelty constantly reminding us of his inconcealable Stalinist roots.

A Few Good Men:

J.F.Kennedy when he assumed power in 1961 as the President of the US, was perceived to be cut from a different cloth from that of his predecessors for his strong pacifist leanings. Just like how Khrushchev had desperately wanted to break away from the past but had ended up being its reluctant captive, Kennedy couldn't help giving in to CIA's aggressive overtures with respect to Cuba which had very recently turned Communist. Fidel Castro, a young and charismatic lawyer-turned revolutionary had managed to liberate Cuba from the clutches of US-supported Franco Batista, the country's much despised dictator in the year of 1959. Cuba, for decades had been ravaged by America's powerful corporations with CIA's help but the sudden emergence of Castro at the helm had changed things overnight. He outlawed these corporations, nationalized all resources, reformed education and subsidised healthcare. When America imposed a trade embargo on Cuba forcing its allies to follow suit, the USSR came to its timely rescue. Trade between the countries flourished and Communist Cuba survived its precarious infancy.

In April 1962, the CIA with the help of Cuban counter-revolutionaries tried to invade Cuba in order to dethrone Castro. Within three days, the Cuban leader had managed to defeat the CIA-supported forces putting Kennedy to terrible shame. The famous (failed) Bay of Pigs Invasion as it is known, enhanced Castro's prestige locally as well as internationally. Probably for the first time in history, the chinks in the mighty American armour had been unveiled and the superpower could no longer be considered completely invincible. Castro took the occasion to forge closer ties with Moscow to safeguard his country in the event of a future American invasion.

As the years passed, Moscow began to take Cuba for granted and started using the island as its backyard. Meanwhile, the US had made arrangements to use Turkey as a base for targeting Russia and had installed Jupiter Intercontinental Ballistic Missiles (ICBM) on the Soviet borders by 1961. Khrushchev, as a countermeasure, had to force Castro to accept stationing of nuclear warheads inside Cuba targeting the US. The US air force sent spy planes over Cuba and confirmed the presence of nuclear missiles to the White House. Kennedy had no other choice but to impose a naval blockade around Cuba to stop the inflow of Russian warheads. Tensions escalated as the Soviet Government informed the White House that a naval blockade will be treated as nothing less than an act of aggression. In a few days, border skirmishes were reported by the Soviet Union and many international leaders were expressing their fears of a full-blown nuclear war. Soon Khrushchev's team was forced to sit down for negotiations with Kennedy's cabinet through a hotline to stop the conflict from getting exacerbated. China's Mao was pressuring Khrushchev to declare war on the US while Kennedy's team was also chomping at the bit to take the USSR head-on. Newspapers all over the world were giving warning signals about the long dreaded nuclear conflict to which the world all of a sudden had come so close. Messages were passed between Khrushchev and Kennedy on a daily basis while the US military was warming up for the finale. Though it is often reported that the USSR was at a huge disadvantage in terms of nuclear strength vis-a-vis the US, Khrushchev had been giving deceptive signals to the world exaggerating Russia's potential manifold.

On October 28, 1962, Kennedy received a letter from Khrushchev offering to withdraw the nuclear warheads from Cuba, provided the former acquiesced to remove the Jupiter missiles from Turkey and Italy. Lyndon B. Johnson, Kennedy's deputy was not willing to take the offer up while top officials at Kremlin were disappointed at Khrushchev for having 'blinked first'. It was so good of Khrushchev to have extended an olive branch first while it was to the great credit of Kennedy to have seized it immediately to make peace.

The tension was defused immediately with both countries taking steps to honour their respective commitments while Cuba's sovereignty was at last recognised by the US the very same year. Even if Khrushchev was riled internally, in hindsight it appears that both the leaders of the power blocs, notwithstanding their political fortunes were clairvoyant enough to stand by peace and save the world from an unimaginably gruesome nuclear armageddon.

CHAPTER VIII

An Unsavory Convergence

One of the most important reasons for me writing this series has been my curiosity to find out why in the 20th century both the Satanic Right Wing and the Messianic Left Wing treated the masses the same way even though their visions were completely different. Through my 6 year old journey with History, I found this question to be extremely intriguing to explore and unravel, and in the upcoming pages I will try my best to get to the root of it.

Theoretical Foundations of the Right:

To find out what underlies the Right wing of the political spectrum, we shall have a look at Nordicism, a racial theory propagated by the Nazis. This theory is strongly built upon the foundation of the inherent supremacy of the White/Nordic/Aryan Race and a strong belief that a society is 'just and natural' only if it obeys the ancient immutable laws of survival. Just like how the lions are at the top of the food chain in a jungle, the Aryans have every right to dominate and enrich themselves at the cost of the lesser races. The lesser races are called so, because they are made of inferior traits such as deceit, stealing, shabby appearances and the like, and contact of the superior races with them shall result in contamination leading to loss of 'racial purity'. If there emerges a condition where intermingling of races is inevitable (as in capitalism), a complete purge of the lesser races is recommended and according to ancient laws, such acts of 'ethnic cleansing' are completely justified.

As you can see, the Right envisions a future 'utopia' where domination of a social group over the other is just the law of the land, in fact of that of Nature, and a society which has unequal access to resources is not only inevitable but also essential for the betterment of the human condition. People who possess a strong belief in these values, who consider contrarian beliefs as nothing less than 'sacrilege' and hence remain impervious and hostile to them, are often called 'fundamentalists'.

Every society which is under flux, at a given instant of time, shall possess both Right-wing or Conservative elements and a completely antithetical set of Left-Wing elements whose mutual interaction or conflict is what we call the progress of human civilization. The Church of the 15th century which strongly abused Copernicus for his Helio-centric model of the Universe can easily be classified as the Right Wing of the medieval Europe while modern inventors like him who challenged traditional belief systems with scientific explanations can be labelled 'Progressive or The Left'.

Needless to say, the colonial ambitions of the Industrial West were strongly bolstered by Right Wing beliefs and the enslaved peoples of Africa and Asia were also made to believe in them. Similarly, the religious orthodoxy of these slave nations was also for the most part, either unmoved by the colonial excesses or fully supportive of it. The very passive role of the Hindu Right in India's struggle for independence serves to exemplify this.

Theoretical Foundations of the Left:

Karl Marx, on the other hand envisioned a future where there is virtually no exploitation of one man by the other, where each individual identifies himself with the rest of the society and where one's aspirations and needs exist in perfect harmony with that of the whole. We call such a future a Communist Utopia where no man is considered to be above the other. Marx was heavily inspired by the Paris Commune experiment of 1871 and wrote extensively about its relevance to contemporary society. His writings spread during the early 20th century and set off movements across the world both in the Industrial West and the colonised East.

The ruling classes all over the world whose domination was sanctified by Right Wing theories had enough reason to feel alarmed. India's freedom fighters of the pre Gandhian era such as Dadabhai Naoroji, Motilal Nehru were directly influenced by international progressive movements which propelled them to construct a comprehensive critique of colonialism whose foundations rested not wholly on sentiments of nationalism, but very substantially on the economic motives underlying imperialism. These leaders were instrumental in the formation of the Indian National Congress in 1885 which in a few decades was to turn into one of the largest mass organisations in the world. In 1927, Brussels in Belgium hosted a conference known as the League Against Imperialism that consisted of leaders of various colonised nations coming together to challenge Western hegemony in Asia (Jawaharlal Nehru was India's delegate) and Africa in a single, unified voice. The League was organised and supported by Communist Russia and in many ways, it served as the precursor to the Non Aligned Movement of 1961 that brought most of the erstwhile colonies under one umbrella.

Leninism vs Marxism:

Communist regimes of the 20th century, it can comfortably be claimed that they were all authoritarian in various degrees, from the sickeningly brutal Stalin's regime to a moderately oppressive one in Tito's Yugoslavia. Hence, even someone who has strong communist inclinations are pushed into the conclusion that both communism and totalitarianism are totally inseparable. However one must remember that since most of the countries of the last century turned communist under strong Soviet influence and had to rely on dictators like Stalin for their survival, repression was pervasive in all countries. This enables us to immediately assume that communism could have been more palatable world over had the Soviet Union not been too intrusive into the affairs of other countries. But it really was not as simple as that.

Pol Pot, the communist leader of Cambodia murdered millions of citizens during his brief period of rule (1975-79) without even an iota of logic. It must be remembered that there wasn't a considerable influence of Soviet Union during the construction of Communist Cambodia and hence very less reason to turn brutal. China too presents a very interesting case where Mao, the founder-leader of the country even though he was considered a theoretician and an independent thinker akin to Vladimir Lenin, on whom the influence of Stalin could only be negligible, also remained a tyrant during most part of his rule. His experiments like the Great Leap Forward and the Cultural Revolution, though they had noble motives ended up swallowing the lives of millions of its citizens. At the root of these experiments, the devilish intent to succeed was exacerbated by a complete disregard for human lives. More cases such as Romania, Poland, East Germany, Ukraine present similar phenomena though levels of repression vary greatly in each one of them.

So we finally see that a communist system as far as it has existed has thrived only under conditions of violence and repression and this leads us to question even the legitimacy of the Marxist doctrine itself. Marx, in his writings had vouched for a brief 'dictatorship of the proletariat' during the Socialist phase of the Revolution. By dictatorship he meant the rule of the working class over the propertied classes which would rearrange the production relations of a society for the better. Marx also had assigned the leadership of the Revolution to the Communist Party which was to serve as the 'vanguard of the proletariat'. The Party was supposed to educate the masses, radicalise the trade unions and peasant organisations and finally lead the struggle against the propertied classes.

But when we look into what happened in Russia, we find that Lenin had actually done the reverse. Firstly, the term 'dictatorship' was taken literally and the phrase 'vanguard of the proletariat' horribly misinterpreted. The 'vanguard of the proletariat' actually meant a group of individuals who best represent the versatile interests of the working classes which determine the pace and the direction of the Revolution. A leadership which does not take into account the aspirations of the proletariat has no right to call itself 'the vanguard'. This naturally means that the Communist Party, the sole representative of the working classes, must function democratically, encourage debate and sufficiently decentralize authority. But what Lenin had created was a coterie of top party members whose elitism was strikingly manifest in what was called 'democratic centralism'. The party elite or the Politburo took decisions on their own, passed orders downward and forced party members to comply. Dissidents were persuaded repeatedly to accept the party line or to leave the organization altogether. The

Politburo had so much condescension for the populace that it believed that the masses had no minds of their own and that it was its bounden duty to educate and guide them to a better future.

Democratic Centralism which was an integral part of Leninism was hence a horrible distortion of the Marxist theory. This kind of practice was propagated to all the satellites of the USSR and other countries as well. Once Stalin assumed power, he applied the theory rigorously on the Soviet society and harvested gruesome consequences. In the process, he also weakened the Politburo by concentrating power into himself and left his successors to inherit the same.

Origins of Tyranny:

Hitler during his formative years had immersed himself in dubious theories of racism and by the time he ascended to the top of the Nazi party, he was already a convinced right-winger. He believed in the distorted interpretations of Nietzsche and Darwin and had wanted to cleanse the society of the taints of inferior races. He sincerely hated Marxism which had vouched for universal brotherhood and felt that it was completely against the Order of Nature. People like Hitler who in some ways are indoctrinated by theories that sound like the 'ultimate truth' psychologically are inclined to believe firmly in their own 'superior' intelligence. Their delusions are so strong and intoxicating that they tend to consider others ignorant and sometimes even superfluous. A similar comparison can be drawn to left wingers who have taken a plunge into Marxist theory. Marxism, as it is widely observed, is a remarkably scientific theory that interprets the whole of human history in quite a meaningful way and gives you the tools to change its future course. It is true that Marxism opens your windows to a wide variety of disciplines that any Marxist scholar will find it difficult to disembark from this extremely liberating intellectual journey. Honestly out of my personal experiences, I strongly feel that Marxism does provide you with a vision of the 'ultimate truth' and it is quite natural that young, fertile minds are instantly smitten by it. However the biggest problem arises when one unwittingly considers himself the Chosen One to realise Marx's vision of Communist Utopia just like how mythological texts sometimes excite an unsuspecting mind into a fit of fanatic euphoria.

It is precisely at that moment, the student of Marxism turns into a fundamentalist by becoming impervious to any kind of contrarian beliefs. It is true that our student has lofty intentions to bring peace and prosperity to one and all, in contrast to his right wing counterpart who believes in the validity of a fractured society, but that doesn't make him any less a fundamentalist. Any kind of fundamentalism instantly breeds intolerance and hatred expecting an abject surrender of the rest of the world towards it. When liberals like us have no compunctions in calling right-wingers as 'bigots' and 'fascists', it is ironic to note that we do not display the same readiness to brand Marxist supremacists like Lenin, Stalin with the same tags. When a particular group considers itself higher than the rest of the society and seeks legitimacy of its authority on account of it, it must be labelled 'fascist' even if its intentions are supposedly noble. And, any kind of fascism, be it religious or intellectual in this case, inherently harbours a contempt towards the innocent masses which morphs soon into despotism whose consequences are everywhere to see.

CHAPTER IX

An Unceremonious End

The world was stunned on October 4, 1957. No country of the first world had managed to achieve this feat. A new age had been heralded by none other than the ''retrograde commies'. There was not much celebration in the CPSU organ Pravda to match the extent of shock and alarm that splashed all over the headlines of Western newspapers. When the Russians had decimated the Nazis in 1945 to seal a glorious victory over the Axis forces, the Western world had been bludgeoned into a humble acknowledgment of the Soviet military might. Even when the Soviet Union was progressing with significant rates of economic growth during the early 1930s, especially when the rest of the world was grappling with negative rates of growth owing to the Depression, the West wasn't quite intrigued about the curious efficacy of the Soviet Model. But by the end of the Second World War, for the Western Elite there was no escaping the fact that there indeed was yet another superpower, this time from the Eastern part of the world. But within two decades of that grand achievement, the USSR had managed to strike again, this time surgically at the heart of the Western pride. Sputnik 1, the first ever man-made satellite was launched successfully into the space from Baikonur, Kazakh ASSR by the Soviet Space Agency. The First Secretary of the CPSU, the then head of the Soviet State, Nikita Khrushchev was named 'Man Of the Year 1957' by TIME magazine the same year.

Goo of good intentions:

Khrushchev wanted to increase the country's agricultural production manifold and ensure self-sufficiency, by vigorously expanding his pet Virgin Lands Experiment. He wanted to divert the humongous amount of funds going into the defence budget towards agricultural and industrial expansion. To minimise defence spending, he went out of his way to warm up to the United States. He brought scientists from Iowa in the U.S to the USSR to set up corn fields and maximise corn production. He increased outlays for fertiliser and pesticide manufacturing and intensified his scrutiny on food production. He opened Party conferences and meetings to the public and ordered dissemination of the proceedings through newspapers and other media. To top it all, he split the party structure into two - one to govern agriculture and the other to control industry.

Khrushchev by 1958, had managed to take control of the entire party by weakening the position of Stalinist leaders. He deposed Bulganin and removed anyone who stood in the way of his well- meaning reform. He amended party laws as to replace committee members periodically at all levels of the organisation. He also worked seriously on the rehabilitation of 'disgraced' party men and officials who fell under Stalin's radar during the Great Terror. But, the saddest part of the story was that none of these moves ended up yielding expected results.

The Virgin Lands project, within a span of five years could no longer sustain the handsome yields that it generated initially. By early 1960s, the project was turning out to be a failure with rapidly dwindling returns. His ambitious corn project and his moves to revamp dairy industry were also not working due to bureaucratic ineptitude and improper planning. His excessive reliance on a genetic scientist Lysenko whose dubious credentials came out only later, for improving the quality of crop output turned out to be a huge mistake. Khrushchev's public denunciation of Stalin embittered many of his own supporters in the party and unwittingly engendered the formation of many powerful rival factions. Most importantly, the bifurcation of the party organisation created completely unforeseen problems. Most of the party cadres working under Khrushchev were not the kind of committed idealists who formed the bedrock of the party during Lenin's time. Ever since Stalin's purges, the composition of the party had been greatly altered with careerists, opportunists and manipulators replacing those selfless partymen and erstwhile revolutionaries who had hitherto occupied higher positions. Khrushchev's plans to periodically replace one-third of the cadre had dented the prospects of them reaching the higher rungs of the organisation while his drastic move to split the party into two was resented deeply almost at all levels. Administratively too, the bifurcation was a great debacle due to an unavoidable overlapping of duties between the agriculture and industry verticals which in turn led to a lot of duplication of functions and tasks.

Finally, Khrushchev's move to reconcile with Kennedy during the Missile Crisis of 1962 was also not appreciated by many of the party's hardliners and his erstwhile supporters. He was soon isolated internally by his estranged colleagues who were waiting for an opportunity to remove him from power.

'I won't put up a fight'

Nikita Khrushchev's approach to other nations was completely contrary to that of his predecessor. He re-established relations with Marshal Tito of Yugoslavia even though the latter was quite reluctant to reconcile. Khrushchev's valuable help to China to build its own nuclear technology was also not sufficiently reciprocated by Mao. China had long before jettisoned the Soviet approach to Socialism and tried to evolve its own model christening it 'Socialism with Chinese characteristics'. In the Indochina crisis involving the United States, Khrushchev wanted to go soft and slow in order to avoid large scale military clashes while Mao remained cold and unyielding. China's aggressive attitude worried Khrushchev terribly and he was pushed to the point of abruptly withdrawing all technical assistance and equipment for the completion of the ambitious Chinese nuclear mission. This was because, Khrushchev believed that an untrammeled Mao, especially at the height of the Indochina crisis would definitely pull the entire world into a nuclear war and hence he did everything in his power to mitigate the situation. He didn't mind drawing criticism from his colleagues and East European counterparts when he visited the United States in 1959 to become the first Soviet leader to do so. He also met J.F.Kennedy at Vienna in 1961 to resolve both the Indochina and Berlin issues amicably.

In spite of his best efforts to cut down military expenditure through negotiations and compromises with the U.S, the situation in Vietnam and Laos worsened during his years taking a heavy toll on the overall Soviet financial health. As his endeavours at expanding agriculture through massive state investments were failing without generating commensurate returns, the USSR had to rely on other countries for food to resolve frequent shortages and famines that were being increasingly reported across the country. His decision to hike the prices of food articles on account of shortages in 1962 led to protests everywhere which had to be put down forcibly.

On October 14, 1964, Leonid Brezhnev leading a powerful team of top leaders bolstered by assured support from all levels of the party, orchestrated a coup quite successfully, by arresting Khrushchev immediately upon his return from vacation, within the premises of the Moscow airport itself. When Khrushchev was confronted by KGB officials, he quickly understood the situation and co-operated with them without raising cries of protest.

Inspite of so many failings and mistakes, the man who was primarily responsible for the De-Stalinisation of the country amid brewing political opposition, the benevolent dictator who managed to improve the living standards of his citizens with his tremendously successful housing scheme, the first leader of the USSR who believed in peaceful coexistence with neighbours and rivals, the enigmatic Nikita Khrushchev, exited the scene after serving as the Head of the State for eleven years. It has been reported that Khrushchev called his ally Anastas Mikoyan during the very night after his ouster and spoke the following words:

"I'm old and tired. Let them cope by themselves. I've done the main thing. Could anyone have dreamed of telling Stalin that he didn't suit us anymore and suggesting he retire? Not even a wet spot would have remained where we had been standing. Now everything is different. The fear is gone, and we can talk as equals. That's my contribution. I won't put up a fight."

CHAPTER X

Smells of Autumn

Alexei Kosygin became the Prime Minister (Chairman of the Council of Ministers) in 1964 immediately following Brezhnev's accession to the top. Kosygin was a technocrat and the new leadership displayed a strong zeal to reform the national industry through technical innovation and suitable administrative re-organisation. Various branches of the industry were allowed sufficient leeway to interact among themselves which Kosygin thought would infuse some dynamism into the processes of production. This move mandated some amount of decentralisation since the State had to pull out of the business of setting production targets. Price controls were moderately relaxed and demand- oriented targets rather than State mandated ones were introduced. The concept of performance based incentive was expanded to all types of industries. The reform introduced in 1965, took some five years to get implemented in full and prospects of improved economic output and better standards of living looked bright.

Costs of Being the Saviour:

Inspite of contradicting estimates from various sources, we can safely assume that the USSR was allocating more than 25 percent of its annual budget towards military expenses post the demise of Stalin. In the post WW2 period, especially after Khrushchev took over, the USSR was only happy to be servicing the needs of the Third World, lending financial and military support to various anti colonial movements against the West. But during Brezhnev's period the conflict between the Western powers and the Vietnamese Communists had intensified and the USSR was obliged to sponsor the latter's campaign, almost fully. The North Vietnamese militia was led by Ho Chi Minh who banked heavily on the support of the Soviet Union both during the First Indochina war against the imperial France and also during the Second Indochina War, also known as the Vietnam War, against the United States-led forces. The war which lasted for more than a decade was one of the bloodiest in history, with Vietnam being pounded by more than four times the total ammunition employed by all the belligerents in the Second World War. Even though the war drained the American economy considerably, the Soviet Union by mid 1970s is reported to have spent close to 7 billion USD to help Communist Vietnam stand and fight on its own legs. As the war drew to a close in 1975 with the defeat of the American forces, the prestige of the Soviet Union as a genuine military superpower, rose higher among the world nations, even though it was purchased at a terribly unsustainable cost to the internal economy.

The Soviets helped in the unification of the whole of Vietnam under Ho Chi Minh, also drawing the smaller nations like Cambodia and Laos into the newly formed Southeast Asian Communist bloc. Brezhnev, even though a Stalinist by principle, was not willing to abandon Khrushchev's efforts to revive domestic agriculture and industry, as a result of which sincere initiatives such as Kosygin's reforms were implemented under his regime. The Soviet society which underwent a massive industrialisation drive under Stalin (at the expense of agriculture) remained a booming economy until the late 1960s, the exact point of inflection in its economic trajectory where the costs of the Cold War were beginning to slowly erode the foundations of the young economy. Also Brezhnev drove the Soviet nuclear program to its logical conclusion by enormously investing in the technology and by the early 1970s, even pro-Western observers grudgingly acknowledged that the Soviet Union had achieved its most coveted nuclear parity with the United States.

Yet, the fact that the USSR remained home to thousands of underfed people who had to wait in long queues to obtain their basic necessities for their day-to-day survival was completely undeniable. All of these realities co-existed with the fact that by the early 1970s, the USSR had grown almost 60 percent to the size of the US economy. But from then on, Brezhnev's rule up to the collapse of the Empire under Gorbachev in 1991, was characterized by economic stagnation and consequent decline.

'You are not him'

A lot of reasons could be attributed to the stagnation and gradual decline of the Soviet economy, one of which was the nature of the Communist Party leadership that had the last word in all aspects of the country's administration. As mentioned earlier, the party composition especially at the top of the pyramid was made up of power-mongers, careerists and even black- marketers during Brezhnev's time. The great revolutionary vision formed and nurtured during Lenin and Stalin's time was completely forgotten in the 1970s and all efforts were concentrated on retaining power for as long as possible. As a result, the ambitious reforms of Kosygin were considerably diluted during the execution phase with the Party officials continuing to prevail over industry managers in the decision-making areas related to material flow, supply and demand management. Managers and higher officials manipulated the incentive system so well that they achieved dramatic revisions in their annual pay every year, while the rest of the workers were left to grapple with increasing prices and stagnating wages. Avenues to innovate were also not sufficiently explored since there were strict limits on R&D investments and very minimal rewards and incentives for successful inventions. Even market-based demand conditions to the extent it was allowed to exist could not bring about improvements in the quality of consumer products that reached the end user.

Secondly, the Soviet Union witnessed massive migration of citizens from rural to urban areas right from the days of Stalin and by the late 1970s, the urban population almost overtook the total number of rural inhabitants. Most of the urban citizens were industrial workers, clerks, office bearers and teachers whose demand for consumer products was growing rapidly year-on-year. These demands could not be met by the supply chains managed by the State which naturally gave way to a booming black economy. Even though its size remains a mystery to everyone, the impact of the black market on the lives of urban citizens was very huge. The existence of the black market and its unstoppable growth stood testimony to the gaping holes in the rusting Soviet command- driven economic model which was on the other hand being massively drained by the Cold War expenses.

And another most important factor that undermined the Soviet economy was the immense desperation that informed the attitude of its leadership towards economic planning, about the need to compete with the United States and stay relevant all the time in the crucial ideological battle. A predominantly agricultural Russia of the 1920s need not have been, at the first place thrust into an agonising industrialisation drive under Stalin that too at such a humongous human and material cost. And the rankling insecurity of the leadership that pushed them to frequently compare the economic indicators of Russia with that of the United States precluded any useful attempt to sincerely study and address the growing demands of its suffering citizens. From my own point of view, it is not a mistake to assume that the United States was a highly industrialised nation right from the 1920s and economic growth of the superpower post the Second World War was driven to a large extent, by bleeding the hapless Third World economies spread across Latin America, Africa and Asia. On the other hand, from sources deemed reliable, it could confidently be stated that the Soviet Union didn't colonise or exploit its East European satellites as much as its Western counterpart did in the resource-rich Third World. Soviet Russia, probably owing to its idealistic roots gave more than what it took from the rest of the world and most of its economic achievements were made possible, unlike its competitor, not because of its aggressive expansionism world over, but wholly inspite of it. Soviet help to Communist China in its infancy is conservatively estimated to exceed 4 billion USD according to various sources while its economic aid to Cuba and younger communist nations like Vietnam, Cambodia, etc is believed to have approached almost the same sum. Needless to say, these were massive transfers of wealth from the USSR to the Third World that were driven mostly by goodwill and ideological commitment that successfully overrode commercial and geo-political considerations.

It is another simple yet elemental fact that seems to have eluded the policy makers of the Soviet Union that their economy was not modelled to survive on profit motives and thrive on concomitant imperialist designs, unlike that of the United States and hence, comparisons of economic growth rates between the two countries were bound to be futile and often highly misleading.

However, the 'Destalinised' Soviet Union having been transformed into a formidable superpower entrusted with 'super' responsibilities which it could not afford shouldering in the long run, soldiered on through the 1970s steadily and uncomplainingly with a brave face. In 1979, Leonid Brezhnev, this time received a call for help from neighbouring Afghanistan ruled by a faction-ridden Communist Party to set its house in order as quickly as possible. The Soviet Politburo that met on December 24, 1979 at Moscow without its Premier Kosygin, reluctantly ordered the immediate sending of troops to Afghanistan. The thickly eye browed Brezhnev reclined on his chair in one of the musty rooms of the Kremlin must have found it hard to conceal the growing wrinkles of worry that were swiftly spreading all over his forehead, soon after he had signed the order. Had the uncannily resilient Soviet Union managed at last, to find a newer road to its destruction?

CHAPTER XI

The Beginning of Autumn

In 1968, the government led by the Communist Party of Czechoslovakia attempted to liberalise the economy through market oriented measures but strictly within the realm of socialism by encouraging worker cooperatives and market pricing guidelines. Freedom of expression was also encouraged which instigated the masses to demand better wages and working conditions. Alexander Dubcek, the then Head of the Czechoslovakian state initiated these reforms against the wishes of the Party orthodoxy. Dubcek was warned several times by Moscow to withdraw the reforms with immediate effect, while civilian protests began to spread all over the country rapidly. Dubcek refused to budge even when other nations of the Warsaw Pact pressurised him to retreat. After a few days, Leonid Brezhnev decided to send troops into Prague to put down the revolt. The reforms were rolled back and Czechoslovakia was shown its place in the East European camp. The Prague Spring of 1968, as it is famously called was instrumental in the formulation of the Brezhnev Doctrine, an agreement which empowered Moscow to interfere into the internal affairs of its satellites whenever a threat to socialist stability and peace was detected.

The Soviet Citizen:

The USSR had completed more than sixty years of socialism by the 1970s and almost a couple of generations of people had been born and brought up in the revolutionary Soviet environment. The repressive nature of the State had during Brezhnev's time been significantly altered and people could manage to lead peaceful lives as long as they did not mess with the government. The Russian citizens, a majority of them though poor by the standards of the West, were assured of free education and healthcare, jobs and employment benefits even if they had to queue up for hours to buy their daily essentials. There were no major famines or large scale shortages of food in the Union post- Khrushchev and most Russians ate sparingly if not better and hunger, it could safely be said was clearly a thing of the Stalinist past. The working conditions of industrial and agricultural labour were far less oppressive than they were during the formative years of the Union and hence getting accustomed to them was not much of a stretch for most of the Russians. A considerable part of the workforce was made of survivors of the Stalinist order and hence they fared much better during the years of Brezhnev. The cultural life of the Russians under Brezhnev was characterized by huge cinema halls featuring old fashioned melodramas, propaganda movies, songs and audio plays broadcasted by the State owned radio. Since there was not much scope for variety entertainment in Russia and also because much of the populace was literate, the Russians had a specially cultivated reading habit that grew very much after Khrushchev's era of Destalinisation. Russians could access literary classics from around the world and those novels from the West which narrated stories about luxurious people and freer societies were also allowed. From a variety of historical sources, it has been borne out that during Brezhnev's era, Russia was the second largest economy in the world and also the largest producer of steel, pig iron, cement and tractors. The Union, in parallel was also subsidising a lot of younger nations ostracised by the rest of the world. In addition to these achievements, the fact that they had been the first ones to enter space was also a matter of great pride for the Russian commoners.

Though there have been a lot of contradictory reports on this, there is a lot of evidence that during Brezhnev's time, the Russians, inspite of harbouring plenty of grudges against the administration were able to adapt themselves to live peacefully under the iron fisted socialist state and even lead contented lives. Even if the veracity of these evidences could be questioned, it has to be admitted that a lot of empires of the past, even if they were deemed large and unwieldy to control, had managed to survive longer than one would naturally assume, not wholly through efficient apparatuses of repression and propaganda, but also to a large measure, by deriving great strengths from the preternatural resilience of their subjects and their phenomenal instinct for survival. But Brezhnev's Russia, unlike that of his predecessors was far less oppressive and more welfarist and hence it becomes easier to believe when one of the recent surveys held post-Soviet Russia concluded that Brezhnev was the most popular leader of the Soviet century.

Reagan's masterstroke:

Leonid Brezhnev, after a prolonged illness died on November 10, 1982 after ruling the USSR for close to eighteen years. Post his demise, surprisingly there was no power struggle for the first time in the history of the state and another sexagenarian leader Yuri Andropov succeeded him. He soon was replaced by Konstantin Chernenko after being in power for close to fifteen months. Under Chernenko the USSR boycotted the 1984 Summer Olympics held at Los Angeles in fitting response to the US boycott of the 1980 Moscow Olympics. 73- year old

Chernenko who spent most of his tenure in hospital receiving treatment died in February 1985. Chernenko's demise gave Soviet Union its youngest Head of State in history, Mikhail Gorbachev who was part of the new reformist guard of the Party.

On the other hand, Ronald Reagan was elected as the President of the United States in 1981. Reagan, often considered an arch-conservative was not willing to continue his predecessor Jimmy Carter's conciliatory attitude towards the Soviets. During the Oil Glut of 1981, he could observe that falling international oil prices had the potential to weaken the economic foundations of the USSR since a major portion of Soviet revenue was dependent on its oil exports. The Soviet intervention in Afghanistan was to a large extent financed by Russia's massive oil fields and Reagan was of the opinion that if the international situation could be exacerbated by increased American spending on the Cold War, on the event of a sudden fall in international oil prices the Soviet economy would instantly collapse and come to a grinding halt. Not surprisingly, Reagan immediately ordered intensification of American involvement in various countries across the globe such as Yemen, Libya, Angola, Indonesia,etc by infusing billions of dollars into proxy wars backing right wing dictatorial regimes and pro-Western militant outfits against local Communists and liberation movements. Reagan's move in 1986 to supply the Afghan Mujahideens with the latest Stinger Anti -Aircraft missile marked a major watershed moment for the Islamists who were caught in a seemingly interminable war with the Soviet army.

In 1986, the Saudi Arabian leaders announced their decision to increase the production of oil in order to bring the prices down. There is some evidence that the CIA forced the Saudis to effect such a move as part of Reagan's anti-Soviet strategy. As expected, international oil prices tumbled and the USSR within months, suffered a terrible resource crunch. Gorbachev had long been a silent critic of the Brezhnev Doctrine and right from his days of assuming office, he was contemplating ways to shelve it once and for all. His focus was on improving domestic industrial production by leveraging the latest available technology and bettering the living standards of the Russians. He realised that the Union was spending close to a quarter of its GDP towards military expenses and was determined to put his foot down as soon as possible. The Oil Shock of 1986 hastened his decision to withdraw from the war in Afghanistan against the rejuvenated Mujahideens and by 1988, the Soviets began to retreat in phases leaving Kabul's PDPA- ledgovernment to fend for itself.

Gorbachev had to accept that the Soviet misadventure in Afghanistan had been a terrible humiliation for the great empire but he believed that there were far bigger embarrassments to deal with. For the first time in Soviet history, the annual economic growth in the mid-1980s was approaching zero, gravely threatening to go negative. Reagan's ploy had worked and Gorbachev had to pull something out of his hat immediately to survive the moment.

In 1987 following the Chernobyl nuclear disaster, the USSR under a dynamic Gorbachev announced a new set of policies namely, 'glasnost' and 'perestroika', which literally meant openness and reform. Unlike that of his predecessors, this time the term 'reform' was meant very seriously. Gorbachev went against the opinions of his colleagues to get them implemented on the ground as quickly as possible. As a result, within a couple of years,

Gorbachev's perestroika was able to produce not only tangible social results and conspicuous economic outcomes but also unforeseen and even perilous consequences that would eventually loom up to swallow the whole of the Soviet Empire itself.

THE INDIAN CONNECTION

Before we venture out to investigate the climactic phases of the Soviet collapse, I really deem it critical to examine the role of Soviet inspired socialist movements in India whose influence on our political and social lives can hardly be exaggerated. The Soviet Union, it must be remembered, was a powerful influence not only over the areas it politically controlled but also over lands and regions which hardly knew nothing more than its name. One such country was India whose course in history was strongly tied to that of the Soviet Union and whose complex relationship with the latter demands a detailed examination that should span at least two chapters from here.

CHAPTER XII

The Socialist South

The first chapter will focus on the South where the Soviet influence was relatively more pronounced while the other chapters will try to give a pan-Indian account of the events. This chapter has additional emphasis on Tamilnadu's politics for obvious reasons.

The October Revolution in Russia succeeded in 1917. The Communist Party of India was formed exactly eight years later. Communist ideas spread like wildfire and socialists proliferated all over India in the 1930s inspired by the tremendous strides made by the Soviet Union's command economy. Jawaharlal Nehru led a very influential faction of Soviet-inspired left wingers inside the Congress party itself. The Congress in 1938 also adopted a resolution to follow a Soviet-style planned economic model once the British Raj was done away with. E.V.Ramaswami, a social reformer who went on to lead the most influential 'Dravidian movement' in Tamilnadu started off as a communist in the early 1920s. The term Revolution which hitherto had not been part of popular parlance anywhere started becoming a household word all over India. Anything that was meant to represent something new and path-breaking was given a 'revolutionary' prefix.

Congress Socialism:

Post-Independence, the first provincial elections held in Madras State gave a clear mandate to a Communist - led alliance. If not for an act of sabotage by the veteran Congressman C.Rajagopalachari, the Communists would have headed the first provincial government of Madras

Presidency. However, that event could do no damage to the growing appeal of socialist ideas all over South India. The Congress Government led by Kamaraj from 1954 followed a welfare model giving prime importance to the growth of education and creation of public sector industries. Natural resources were nationalised, public schools with mid-day meal scheme were opened all over, public distribution system to redistribute grain was created and strengthened. In parallel, the Dravidian ideologues who dominated the heights of the booming Tamil cinema industry ensured that the 'bourgeois' elements of the society were identified with the Congress party as a whole and portrayed the party in poor light through films that appealed to the nationalistic pride of Tamil speakers. Akin to Soviet propaganda films that usually showed scheming landlords and nobles being trumped in the end by impoverished workers, Tamil cinema too churned social dramas, historical films that shed light on the plight of the toilers, women exploited by rich men and landlords, religious godmen misusing the faith of the believers to amass fortunes, etc.

Trade unions mostly affiliated to the Communist parties spread across industrial towns and left-wing peasant societies that fought caste, class and gender inequalities multiplied across rural South India. Militant left wing groups proliferated across Kerala and Telangana regions especially where caste exploitation was at its peak. Upper caste landlords whose excesses remained unchecked by successive Congress governments were eliminated by Communist insurgent groups and land redistribution programmes were implemented. When EMS Namboodiripad headed the world's first democratically elected Communist Government in Kerala in 1957, a massive land reform programme to eliminate caste and class exploitation was launched. Kerala's education which was hitherto dominated by land-owning Christian orthodoxy was brought under the purview of the State Government. Meanwhile lands under Hyderabad Nizam's suzerainty were liberated by Communist militants and redistributed to Telangana peasants.

Communists lose to 'Socialism':

In 1967, a left wing coalition government headed by the DMK dethroned the Congress Government in Tamilnadu and initiated another round of welfare measures. Land reform was implemented (whose rate of success was very questionable) for the first time in Tamilnadu. Hindu temples that owned huge acres of land were nationalised, primary education system was strengthened and a slew of redistributive schemes were initiated. The more the DMK moved leftward in the political spectrum inspite of rampant institutionalised corruption, the more marginalised the mainstream communist parties became in Tamilnadu. Their electoral fortunes steadily dwindled as the DMK soon split into two, giving rise to a newer bloc led by cinema superstar MG Ramachandran in 1972. MGR, as he was affectionately called was the poster-boy of the Dravidian movement right from its days as a mass organisation. One of the most important reasons why Tamilnadu turned leftward moving more and more along Dravidian lines was the popularity of MGR whose public image was built strongly around the ideas of socialism and egalitarianism. He often played in his films, the champion of the working classes who had the rare guts to question the villainous landlords and other rapacious vested interests. Most of his songs that outlived his time had great music and crowd pleasing social messages which played a critical role in disseminating Dravidian propaganda among the masses. As mentioned earlier, the Dravidian movement popularised the idea of calling newer and radical things 'revolutionary' hoping to steal some of the magic the October Revolution had created across the world and MGR was called 'revolutionary leader' by his fans on his road to becoming the first cinema star to get elected as the Chief Minister of a state in 1977.

The split of the DMK into two led to two important far reaching consequences. One, the quality of Soviet inspired welfarism soon deteriorated into becoming a model of corruption-driven populism where people were continually kept in the thrall of poverty while simultaneously being fed with a slew of State sponsored freebies that ranged from food-grains to consumer durables. Two, with the appearance of newer actors in Tamilnadu politics, the mainstream Left shrunk terribly losing huge chunks of its electoral support to its pseudo-socialist rivals. The Left however continued to dominate mass organisations such as trade unions and peasant societies as a result of which workers and farmers in Tamilnadu managed to achieve reasonable standards of living through continuous struggles for better wages and living conditions.

Moribund communism:

As the century drew nearer to a close, Tamilnadu owing to its successive welfarist governments led by both the Dravidian parties had above average literacy rates, better roads and infrastructure and decent health standards, all of which came in good stead, when in 1991, India moved towards a market-driven industrial economy. Multinational corporations which saw cheap labor in India gravitated more towards the South than the North for want of better technical skills and systematised professional education in order to establish factories, software development centres, export processing units,etc in its huge well-maintained urban areas. Cities such as Chennai, Bangalore, Coimbatore grew into industrial hubs under the aegis of the State thereby providing well-paying jobs to millions of people who in turn moved swiftly along the economic ladder. A newer middle class which was the immediate beneficiary of the trickle-down market economy expanded in size greatly and promptly lost all its formative allegiances to socialist movements and ideas. The mainstream Left parties which had ceded their space to pseudo- socialist forces during TN's pre-liberalisation era, by early 2000s had almost been completely excised from the political discourse of the state which was now increasingly being dictated by the new, aspirational, cosmopolitan middle class that ironically prided itself on its fashionable 'political ignorance'.

The unravelling of the mainstream Left in Tamilnadu (and even in Andhra) had plenty of reasons. Firstly, the Left parties were hugely dependent on meagre donations and contributions from its party cadre, union members and common people for their day-to day organizational expenditure. As the size of the election market grew with time its rival parties were able to rake in millions from their rich patrons and corrupt practices while being in power. Hence the perennially penurious Communists logically stood no chance against their cash-rich rivals who were only quite happy to co-opt them into their temporary electoral alliances. Secondly, the Left parties could not find ways and means to sensitise their own union workers and peasants on class issues and offer lasting solutions to their day-to-day problems. As a result, even members belonging to the Left wing trade unions cared less to vote for the party during the elections, making use of their organised strength solely to achieve quick fixes for daily problems within and outside their workplace. Thirdly, in the era of liberalisation, the free market had infused a completely different socio-cultural outlook on its people where careerism, consumerism and an all pervasive fear of survival easily trumped Independence-era virtues such as idealism, sacrifice, social awareness and moral anger. In addition, the abrupt collapse of the Soviet Union in 1991 confused the ideological core of the party who suddenly couldn't respond adequately to questions doubting the validity of their founding theories. A terribly confounded party elite mired in self-doubt such as this one, must have found it difficult to pass their rich theoretical inheritance to their next generation who naturally could have mustered no inclination to dabble in them. An intellectually vapid Left party not only impoverishes the society it inhabits but also receives in return, ignorant and ideologically bankrupt cadre into its fold who complete a self-reinforcing cycle of intellectual scarcity and never-ending knowledge drought.

Kerala, Soviet Union's last relic:

However, Kerala owing to its completely unique socio-economic history went through a remarkably different political journey from that of its neighbouring Tamilnadu. The early advent of Christian missionaries into Kerala, the swift conversion of Hindu lower castes into Christianity and Islam, rapid spread of education through missionary owned schools, extreme oppression of lower caste peasants by their upper caste landlords and other crucial factors mined the soil for the sprouting of militant insurgency movements led by Soviet inspired Communists all over Kerala. Communists bore the brunt of the excesses unleashed by landlord-police nexus before and after independence which fortunately gave them a great electoral advantage over that of their opponents. Kerala was the first state in India to vote for a non-Congress government in 1957 and the state made great progress in health, education and sanitation indices.

Communists played a significant role in deepening of democracy in Kerala by empowering panchayati institutions and local civic bodies. Agricultural and industrial cooperatives encouraged by the State brought workers and farmers together in great numbers cutting across rigid caste and religious divisions. Implementation of government schemes were spearheaded by party cadre and local masses which played a great role in effectively rooting out bureaucratic and political corruption. Kerala became the first state to achieve 100 percent literacy in the country and also remains the only state in India to have more females than males.

However such a climate where the masses played an active role in political affairs, was not considered suitable for industry by investors when India moved towards a market economy in 1991. Kerala's economy it must be admitted was considerably dependent on its massive diaspora housed in the faraway Gulf in spite of concerted efforts by the State to build strong co-operative and public sector industries. Without proper federal autonomy, no government could aspire to create a self-reliant state economy in a diverse country such as India. State governments, as is the case with the rest of India need to keep appealing to the Centre for funds time and again and hence building an industrial economy without the participation of the local private sector by the State government is close to impossible.

In today's scenario, on one hand, a young and an aspiring urban middle class in Kerala taught by a heavily regulated pro-poor state education system, and one that was weaned on massive remittances from the Gulf slowly gravitates towards a powerful Hindu Right that emerges on the promise of high paying jobs, glitzy malls and gated communities through market-driven economic policies. While on the other, the lower classes keep favoring the traditional welfare economy built by Left and local Congress governments in election after election.

However, Kerala remains the only state in India which continues to buck the nationwide trend in more ways than one. It keeps recording the highest levels of Human Development indicators in India year on year competing with the great Industrial West on almost all of them. On a similar note, it is the only place in India which still holds the ideas of Marx and Lenin close to its heart even after 27 years of the collapse of the Soviet Union, at a curious time when the rest of the country is fast unmooring itself from its benevolent legacy.

CHAPTER XIII

Eastern Promises

India's political economy was marked to head leftward even before its birth. The scars of English Imperialism were fresh and festering and the Congress think tank led by the visionary statesman, Jawaharlal Nehru had no other choice but to go socialist. The alternatives provided by the neighbouring USSR were too tempting to resist - by early 1950s the Soviet empire had revived spectacularly inspite of the devastating effects of the Second World War. Planned economy and a pro-poor welfare model summarised Nehru's vision for India and he set out in that direction in spite of forces pulling him from behind and sideways.

The Communist Party of India by 1948 had called for an armed insurrection against the 'bourgeois' government led by Nehru and he responded just like every other national leader would do when faced with violent internal upheaval - deploying large scale repression. He was helped on this count enormously by Sardar Patel whose contempt for left wingers was widely known. The CPI, unable to withstand severe state retaliation, was literally decimated within a few months mainly due to lack of popular support coupled with poor understanding of Indian conditions. The loss sustained by the left was very huge which in turn reflected in the forthcoming elections. The rank and file too felt demoralised and the backfiring of their armed tactics sapped all their revolutionary vigor.Still, the party remained the second largest political outfit in India even after losing a huge chunk of its cadre to governmental repression.

Communists brace for a split:

Jawaharlal Nehru emphasised the role of the State in managing the affairs of the national economy and his government set out to establish a lot of public sector industries whose contribution to nation-building turned invaluable in the upcoming decades. Agriculture was given prime importance in the inaugural five year plans and India's agricultural production doubled and trebled in the 1960s. The industrial output also grew manifold which in turn spurred a staggering revival of the Indian economy for the first time post-Independence. Living standards of Indians also rose as a result of which questions about national unity and social cohesion post liberation were put to rest. Secularism was firmly drilled into the minds of Indians and national elections proved time and again that a majority of Indians identified themselves firmly with the idea of India despite racial and linguistic differences.

The Communists too were impressed by the progress India was making, guided by socialist ideals and Leninist principles of economic planning while, in parallel, disillusionment spread among a few left wing groups whose dream of a complete socialist revolution was rapidly fading. These groups were not quite wrong when they observed that the Congress, inspite of Nehru's efforts was increasingly falling prey to the designs of India's reactionary classes and acting by and large against the will of the poor majority. A large number of Congress legislators and parliamentarians hailed from the wealthy upper castes and did everything in their power to block Nehru's ambitious land reform programme. As a result, land reforms all over India were only marginally successful and in rural areas, wealth distribution continued to be skewed in favour of the traditional elites. Tensions simmered between landlords and lower caste peasants even into the 1960s since governmental efforts to improve the lives of the latter were not bearing much fruit.

Communists divide yet rule:

Nehru's ground-breaking policy of international non-alignment was a tremendous success all over the Third world. The relationship of China, India's communist neighbour with its progenitor, the USSR was souring steadily while Chinese leader Zhou En Lai joined Nehru at the Bandung Conference in 1955. China and India had petty border disputes ever since the birth of the republics but Nehru's anti-American attitude which manifested in his efforts to get China a permanent seat in the United Nations helped in minimising tensions for a while. The USSR was also impressed with India's antipathy towards the West and helped the fledgling nation with massive economic and technical assistance. In its wars with Pakistan, the USSR steadfastly supported India in various international forums and assisted it militarily. But in 1962, China stunned Nehru by crossing the frontier and attacking Indian outposts. It is reported that Nehru was not informed properly about the deteriorating situation in the Aksai- Chin border and that his excessive reliance on Chinese goodwill was responsible for poor Indian preparations against the sudden Chinese onslaught. The conflict lasted close to a month and India had to cede a part of the disputed territory to the Chinese.

The impact of the Indo-Chinese conflict was felt nowhere as heavily as on the ranks of the Communist Party. A faction of the party ever since Independence had always taken a more benign view of the Congress and had trusted the grand old party in its ability to take India in a socialist direction. In fact, the party sent a few of its ideologues to infiltrate the Congress echelons and covertly influence policymaking. This faction supported India during the Indo-China war while the rest of the party wavered in its stance. The latter in less than two years broke away from the parent organisation forming the hugely influential Communist Party of India (Marxist) in 1964. The new party was considered to have stronger and more radical leaders than its parent and its influence spread all over West Bengal. During the days of Siddharth Shankar Ray's chief ministership in West Bengal (1972-77), Marxist militants and activists proliferated all over the rural agricultural regions trying to liberate the peasants from the excesses of landlords. Ray taking cue from Patel's methods in curbing communist insurgency indulged in extreme methods of repression that easily overstepped the bounds of constitutionality. Thousands of communists, innocent peasants and farm workers were arrested, assaulted and killed during Indira Gandhi's emergency (1975-77).

However, Ray's tactics backfired when the Left Front swept the assembly polls in 1977. Bengal within a few years showed the way for the rest of the country on implementation of the land reform programme and Jyoti Basu's efforts as Chief Minister in breaking the hegemony of feudal landlords over the traditionally oppressed peasants and workers won plaudits from activists all over India.

Relative Tranquility (1977-2008):

After CPI(M)'s victory in West Bengal in 1977, the Indian mainstream Left, it could safely be stated, attained a period of relative stability in their fortunes for the next three decades or so. Naxalism on the other hand, which originated in the late 1960s as a result of CPI(M)'s split with its radical Leninist sibling was confined within extremely backward rural areas in West Bengal, Andhra Pradesh and Bihar. However within years, the Left had surprisingly developed an easy relationship with electoral politics and their frequent alliances with bourgeois parties appeared more expedient than genuinely idealist. The radicalism of the early 1920s too, was fast disappearing even among the Communist elite and disenchantment within both the left parties kept surfacing time and again in the form of increasing splinter groups and expelled intellectuals. The Left parties however, were able to secure a minimum of 40 seats in the Lok Sabha during every subsequent general election which gave them substantial leverage with respect to policy-making and implementation. The numerous trade unions and peasant societies, under the huge Communist umbrella benefited a lot during this period owing to considerable left-wing presence in the Parliament.

Indira Gandhi's emergence as the most powerful leader in the post-Nehruvian era continued to give hopes to the survival of socialism in Indian policy-making. The abolition of privy purses and nationalisation of banks in the late 1960s, both of which significant advances in the socialist direction drew the admiration of the Left parties. Indira always ensured that her political rhetoric morphed easily into a mythical battle between the left and the right- she representing the pro-poor Good and her opponents belonging to the anti-poor evil camp. However she was extremely careful as not to allow the struggle to blow up into a full-scale class conflict and hence used the Emergency as a means to blunt the edges of both the right and left wing elements in the country. Her unexpected assassination in 1984 marked a significant turnaround in the direction of Indian political economy. As the rest of the world under the influence of Reagan-Thatcherite ideas was unmooring itself from welfare legacies inspired by Keynesianism, India too made use of the opportunity of Indira's demise to move towards the right. Rajiv Gandhi and subsequent leaders of the Congress, moderated now and then by countervailing forces of left-wing trade unions and mass organisations paved the ground for economic liberalisation in 1991.

A peek into the organs and journals of the left parties that were published during this era offers stunning predictions on the future impact on India's polity and the impending aftermath of its move towards economic liberalisation. The Left parties had continued to warn as early as in the 1990s, about a possible collapse of India's agricultural sector in the event of a reform-driven State withdrawing itself from the market. Warnings about unsustainable levels of economic inequality, unmanageable levels of crime as a result, corporate plunder of India's natural resources and irreversible alienation of Adivasis and tribals from their traditional habitats, possibilities of disturbances from Islamist-Wahabbist armed groups in the event of India's embrace of Hindutva nationalist ideas, perils of getting entangled into the sticky web of international economy all of that which sound eerily prescient today appear all over left-wing journals and organs during this period. Calls for action against black money stashed in tax havens abroad and their deleterious effects on Indian economy can be found in press statements issued by left wing leaders as early as in the 1990s.

Left wing governments in Bengal, Kerala and Tripura continued to implement welfare schemes in their respective states even after India's embrace of neoliberalism. Tripura, under the Left Front Government for close to 25 years made great strides similar to Kerala in terms of education and health. It became the first state in the North-East to get rid of the draconian AFSPA law whose repeal was an indicator of political stability forged by the weakening of local partisan and secessionist forces. In the 2004 general elections, the Left parties recorded their highest tally in the Lok Sabha and made a post poll alliance with the Congress -led UPA to keep the Hindu-nationalist BJP out of power. They were instrumental in bringing about the biggest flagship programme in neoliberal India, the National Rural Employment Guarantee programme which ensured a minimum of 100 days of employment in rural areas. Their influence also significantly slowed down the reform-oriented UPA government's attempts to sell public sector companies to private entities and also played a major role in keeping rising petrol prices in check.

You Reform, You Die:

The Left Front Government in West Bengal by late 2000s was drawing immense flak from various quarters for not having nurtured a business-friendly climate in the State even after being in power for close to three decades. The criticism initially was not taken seriously by Jyoti Basu when he was in power but his successor, an irked Buddhadeb Bhattacharya wanted to respond differently. He invited the Tatas to invest in Bengal and assured support to them in issues of land acquisition. The Bengal farmers most of whom were beneficiaries of Basu's land reform were not quite receptive to the government's idea. They resisted land acquisition egged on by rural Maoist and other opposition forces causing great embarassment to the 'reformed' Communist leadership. Confused as to how to respond to public outcry against its pro-business measures, the Left

Front Government suppressed public agitation violently in 2007. Inside a province whose people were known for their hostility towards big business houses and corporate entrepreneurs, a curious attitude which was sowed and cultivated by the incumbent government itself for more than three decades, this move to violently suppress legitimate dissent amounted to nothing less than political suicide. In the 2009 general elections, following the UPA-Left divorce in the Centre on the contentious Indo-US nuclear deal, the Left parties suffered a major electoral reversal in West Bengal. Their tally, as a result shrunk to 29 in the Lok Sabha, their lowest ever in post-Nehruvian India. In the subsequent assembly and general elections, the Left suffered massive losses in Bengal and in the last ten years or so, their shocking obliteration from Bengal's memory appears to be almost complete. Having been unable to expand beyond their limited frontiers, the Left parties have been marginalized effectively from India's electoral arena and subsequently from the nation's political discourse as well.

A cut above the rest:

The reasons for the Left's decline are quite obvious and have been sufficiently discussed in the previous chapter. Here I would like to discuss the legacy of the Left in India which has for the most part either been continuously misrepresented or grossly underreported. The Left movement, it must be noted, played a key role in India's freedom struggle and sacrificed thousands of its rank and file to the cause. All over rural India, they were the first people to raise their voices against centuries-old hegemony of the upper castes and traditional elites over the poor and underprivileged. They played an indispensable role in the deepening of democracy in a feudal, strife-torn, backward

India and in propagating the values of European enlightenment such as secularism, free speech and social equality among the masses.

Post-Independence, their armed as well as peaceful struggles against local elites and capitalists ensured that the peasants and workers were able to improve their working conditions and standards of living significantly. Their mass organisations brought forth both illiterate and poor women from the working classes and allowed them to occupy top leadership and administrative posts. In both Bengal and Kerala, panchayati raj institutions received a major boost under Left rule as a result of which women were represented adequately in local bodies. Most importantly, the Communists' role in preserving India's secular identity amid frequent communal clashes and ever-rising identity politics cannot be overstated.

Having spent close to 70 years both at the heart and periphery of India's electoral polity, the Left still preserves the distinction of being the only mainstream political outfit in the country to remain untainted by scandals or political corruption. Most of the leaders of the Left have remained paragons of personal virtue, leading simple and selfless lives. In addition, it can safely be said that the number of intellectuals, academicians and scholars in the Communist fraternity alone might easily outnumber those belonging to rest of all the political parties put together. The fact that both Bengal and Kerala produce the finest works in various cultural and artistic disciplines and the deep entrenchment of communism in the socio-cultural landscape of both the states are not mere coincidences.

In today's neoliberal India, the crusade of the Communists against class and caste exploitation are not over yet. In the hills and forests of deep interior

Chattisgarh, where the Indian Army siding with the state-sponsored terrorist outfit Salwa Judum take on thousands of poor and landless tribals and Adivasis to chase them away from their traditional habitats in favour of huge mining corporations eyeing India's largest deposits of bauxite and minerals, it is the Communist militants (Maoists) who are at the forefront of the struggle working tirelessly to restore the land to whom it rightfully belongs. As novelist Jeyamohan writes in his blog, no other party or movement is as dedicated and committed to the cause of the poor and underprivileged as the Left in India. Whatever may be their flaws, tactical failures and historical blunders, it is not an exaggeration to say that amid the multitude of parties mushrooming here and there in India's democratic polity every now and then, there are genuinely only two types of political organisations in India - the Left and the rest.

THE WITHERING AWAY AWAY

OF THE STATE

CHAPTER XIV

What did the Soviet Union mean?

When the USSR was created in 1922 there could be no ambiguity about how the citizens felt about it. Most of the peasants, workers and artisans were delighted at being part of a historic civilizational advance, something other nations were not capable of doing. A majority of them hoped for better lives and an atmosphere full of promise and optimism about the future pervaded all through the empire. Lenin however was more a practical man than a romantic visionary, who kept emphasizing the enormity of the obstacles in place towards their march to socialism. He kept telling people that they may have to make huge sacrifices at least in the short term to rearrange the existing production relations as to achieve a reasonable measure of egalitarianism. And people were ready to work for him as millions joined the Red Army to serve their new found Fatherland during the immediate Civil War. Even after Lenin ordered the temporary withdrawal of personal freedoms putting some kind of a martial law in place, there wasn't much of discontent or collective resistance initially. Soon after Stalin's arrival at the scene, the lives of ordinary Russians, it must be admitted was fast turning from bad to worse.

From the late 1930s to the beginning of the World War ll, Russians lost more than they gained as a whole new autocratic order at the top which ensured national stability and internal peace found expression. The new order had in a few years turned robust and implacable and it cannot be denied that most Russians were found vacillating between feelings of loyalty to their ruthless regime and those of disillusionment at the exacting demands and sacrifices it mandated from the ordinary citizens. As the empire entered the War, Stalin's appeal to the masses to protect their country from the aggression of the enemy was accompanied by relaxation of restrictions in personal freedoms and rights. Russia's losses in the War were humongous and almost all revolutionary energy of the masses had been drained at the end of it. However, Russia's victory in the war was incredible even if it was pyrrhic and Stalin tried to capitalize on this success to revive the nation's sagging spirit. The country was back to square one not only in terms of economic standards but also in those of personal freedoms and human rights. Another stunning revival of economy was achieved under a dying yet still enormously charismatic Stalin by which time the people had gotten used to the Stalinist order, which was quite similar to their days under the Tsars.

Khrushchev's time was a period when the average Russian was at last granted the freedom to breathe easy and a similar state of things followed under a harmless Brezhnev. By the middle of Brezhnev's reign, Russia had changed beyond recognition from a feudal, semi-industrial backward country not quite distinguishable from an Asiatic monarchy into a modern, industrial power which could talk in equal terms with the Western superpowers. The standards of living under the Bolsheviks were ordinary compared to the West but much better than those under the Tsars. Millions of peasants and artisans and labourers had access to free and compulsory education, reasonable healthcare and sanitation. The centuries-old bondage to land and primitive identities had been irretrievably broken and most Russians had transformed themselves into clerks, engineers, industrial workers, teachers, etc. Even though Russia was still less free compared to its Western competitors, the loyalty of the citizens to the establishment was by this time quite unquestionable. All this is a way of deflating a huge and baseless lie seeded and nourished by a treacherous and an incurably hostile Western capitalist media that almost all Russian citizens hated the Bolsheviks and were waiting to break into a new, luxurious and advanced life that modern capitalism apparently had the potential to provide.

An incredible story of contradictions:

As many of you would have noted, the purpose of this series is not either to justify what the Communists did for and outside Russia or to debunk the million myths that they dispensed unconscionably about the state of USSR's internal affairs every now and then. In addition, I have no intention to boast of my ability to give a balanced judgement about the Soviet Empire due to the enormous subjectivity involved in this debate. As mentioned earlier, my attempt to revisit the story of the Bolshevik Empire grew solely out of a deep intrigue on account of its unprecedented singularity of character whose flaws and achievements contest each other vigorously in magnitude in almost every single dimension of it.

USSR was the first state in the world to owe allegiance to the glorious tenets of Marxism and hence it is reasonable for any student of history to expect a modicum of equality, freedom and opportunity to live a good life in such an avowedly 'utopian' environment. But unfortunately, USSR came nowhere near it. The Empire curtailed all existing freedoms, swelled concentration camps and institutionalized them, confiscated property, obliterated dissent, justified famines and their mishandling. Just when we smell the shades of a theocratic state or one of a Fascist kind in its aforementioned characteristics, all of a sudden, a wholly new progressive facet is revealed to us. Russia was the first country in the world to establish 'full employment' something the capitalist nations simply did not have the capacity to achieve. The Tsarist Russian society of the 1900s had almost nothing to do with that of the 1960s with almost all of the populace well entrenched into modern institutions of political economy, a transformation which took centuries for the Europeans to achieve. The USSR, it cannot be denied was the first country to achieve another great revolutionary milestone, namely the liberation of women, something which is still a pipedream in many supposedly progressive nations. The Bolsheviks were the first to introduce maternity leave, legalize divorce and provide for equal pay for women with men. Crèches abounded in Soviet Russia and female participation in work was quite the norm than exception.

As historian Isaac Deutscher notes in his book, the Stalinist administration inherited all the feudal traits of Tsarist Russia but, by providing its citizens with formal and professional education along with compulsory studies in Marxism, it unwittingly sowed the seeds for its own downfall. Modern historians have a tendency to compare and equate 20[th]century dictators like Stalin and Hitler so as to denounce the former vehemently with a hidden motive to undermine the appeal of Communism altogether. However, one needs to concede that the magnitude of Stalin's crimes against humanity cannot be considered to be lesser or insignificant in comparison with that of Hitler. Stalin emerges a better ruler than Hitler only if we consider other facets of his administration. Hitler's government thrived largely on racist hatred, propagated and amplified it with a view to creating a highly fragmented society to the point of permanent irreversibility. Stalin's regime on the other hand worked with a single minded efficiency to push the society in the very opposite direction- towards obliterating all primitive identities and divisions and creating a permanently unified whole. Needless to say, Hitler's dividing mission failed soon after it took off while Stalin's mission was a grand success which could have been all the more glorious had it been achieved without shedding human blood and devouring the lives of millions of innocents.

It is also often argued by many intellectuals that Hitler succeeded in transforming a weak and demoralized Germany into a powerful, industrial nation within a span of less than a decade thereby providing millions of jobs to its impoverished workforce, something which his predecessors couldn't achieve. By exaggerating the exploits of Hitler, there is often a spurious attempt to belittle the socialist achievements of the USSR. It is worth reiterating the fact that Germany was the most industrialized nation in Europe even before the beginning of the 20[th]century. Even Marx and his followers including Lenin strongly believed that Germany shall be the first nation in the world to go socialist given the massive industrial advancement it had made during the industrial revolution. So when Hitler took the country over in 1933, he was only improving what was already there in Germany in complete contrast to the backward state of Soviet Russia. Also Germany's industrial development was based largely on the armament industry whose functioning was in turn totally dependent on the prospects of Germany's war making abilities. A lot of economists agree on the fact that Germany's remarkable economic progress owed a lot to Hitler's mission to complete his revenge on its rivals who forced the Versailles' treaty down its throat. Nazi Germany survived on what was called a War Economy which would have collapsed completely during peacetime.

In contrast, Stalinist Russia within less than a decade was showing signs of competing with advanced industrial nations including the United States. Just when its prospects were looking up, the USSR was thrust into one of the most devastating conflicts in human history. The USSR endured a massive human and economic catastrophe in the course of the war and within a decade after winning it, orchestrated a stirring resurgence under Stalin's leadership to catch up with its Western rivals. Any open minded historian of the twentieth century would agree to the fact that no other nation in the world could have sustained such massive economic reversals, remain unmoved and exhibit such uncanny resilience to restore itself to normalcy. During Khrushchev's period in the 1960s, the industrial output of the USSR was fast catching up with that of the United States.

However, the more we tend to attribute these achievements to Stalin, we simultaneously fail to acknowledge the Russian commoner on whose spirit and sacrifice the entire socialist edifice stood proudly for more than four decades after the war. And it is also absurd to argue that the Russians fought for their Fatherland, gave their lives willingly and worked tirelessly to build socialism solely due to coercion and state repression. Numerous accounts including the recent book by Svetlana Alexevitch gives evidences of how committed Soviet Russians were to the cause of their nation and towards building socialism. In various places of the book, Svetlana brings out the stark differences in attitude between erstwhile Soviet citizens and those of today. The citizens of today's capitalist Russia are mocked constantly by their predecessors who lived under socialism for having bonded themselves to cheap things such as careers and commodities for their survival. War veterans and teachers and industrial workers under Soviet Russia proudly boast about living for an 'ideal' (socialism) ridiculing the state of affairs under the new capitalist order.

Svetlana's account adds weight to various assumptions that revolve around today's elderly Russians, a majority of whom feel 'nostalgic' about the Soviet Union. Those, whom Svetlana interviewed, one can observe, vent their frustration of having been betrayed by those who vouched and campaigned for the dismantling of Soviet Russia in promise of freedom and democracy. Most Soviet Russians strongly believed that with the arrival of perestroika and glasnost, there would be more press freedom, an increased participation of citizens in the administration of the state and gradual easing of norms with respect to their interaction with the 'outside'. But what happened within less than half a decade was the establishment of a completely alien free-market economy controlled by local and foreign vested interests in collusion with new oligarchs bent on looting Russia and its satellites. Russian citizens who were used to having access to free education, healthcare and cheap housing with 'decent' employment under socialism were suddenly asked to hurry and join the race for saving their livelihoods. They were asked to adapt immediately to the requirements of the all-new laissez faire order, learn new skills including deceit and subterfuge and familiarize themselves with the new rules of hitherto unknown 'rat-race'.

Making sense of the Soviet Experiment:

Just before I rest my case, I wish to give an honest and concise account of what I personally feel in conclusion, about the strange story of the Soviet Union. Just when I was introduced to the phenomenon of the Soviet Union in my childhood through the kaleidoscope of Communist propaganda with the help of my father, I was deeply enamored of its achievements and promises. As years passed, I learned through capitalist media and its propagandists about the ghastly crimes that had been committed inside the Empire. Honestly I was horrified and the more I learned of them through the lenses of various intellectuals and historians, all I felt was an inner revulsion against the Communists and their shameless instinct for concocting lies and falsehoods. This was the time I was also let into reading Marxist texts and the theoretical foundations of socialism. Needless to say, the theoretical soundness of the Marxist principles and its ability to objectively critique the phenomenon of capitalism fascinated me. By this time, my revulsion for the Communists and their propaganda organs had been mildly softened but something about the vast crevice between their theory and practice kept me both intrigued and appalled. My intrigue grew when I started studying Russian history from sources belonging to various schools of political thought and the irreconcilable contradictions I noted from various perspectives only ended up sharpening my obsession with the story of Soviet Russia.

So how do I make sense of it? Let me put my facts up front. Soviet Russia killed millions of its own citizens. The Communist Party ate millions of its own dedicated cadre. For what one might ask? Did the Soviet leaders amass huge fortunes from the toils and blood of ordinary Russians? No. Or atleast did they achieve Socialism? Well not exactly.

They came close. Oh, does it matter one might ask. Socialism at the cost of millions of lives? Yes it really does not matter. If Socialism can be achieved only through the slaughter and uprooting of millions of lives, let us say a resounding No to Socialism. But is Socialism only that? Killing millions, socializing poverty, expropriating personal freedom and property? Certainly no. Then what do we conclude about it? Do we accept it or reject it?

A tiny humanist lurking beneath the writer in me shakes and cowers at the horror of what happened in the Soviet Union under Stalin. Had I been given a chance to live under such conditions I would surely have opted myself out. But when I go through the record of what you call the Free Market which is often touted to be the alternative for socialism, all I get is nothing less than the proverbial chill down my spine. If you don't believe me, kindly leaf through the histories of Latin America and Africa about how capitalism butchered and enslaved millions of innocent citizens in the name of progress and development in the last few centuries. If you don't have time, kindly read about books on our own experience under the freedom-loving Brits.

So here is my closing statement. Socialism did kill millions of human lives in the USSR mercilessly. During Stalin's regime, the government was one huge irrepressible killing machine. But once you are done shrinking at the horror of what happened out there, open your closed eyes. Enlighten yourself to the fact that Socialism also saved millions and millions of lives across the globe at the same time from the ravages of imperialist capitalism. It gave hopes to multitudes of toiling masses and helped them fight their righteous fight against predatory capitalism. Even today, things we take for granted such as legally guaranteed working hours, pensions, provident fund, maternity leave, voting rights, the right to organize, the right to education, food and a decent living owe their origins to the idea of Socialism. The USSR regardless of how close it came to achieving Socialism internally, was viewed all over the world by the ruling classes as nothing less than a living embodiment of Socialism, an idea that simply horrified them. It was that fear, that terrible fear to protect themselves from the hegemony of the working classes that Socialism stood for, that forced them to grant all the rights and freedoms that you enjoy today. Let that sink in.

CHAPTER XV

The Implosion

The Treaty of 1922 on the Creation of the USSR was concluded by the heads of the Russian, Ukrainian, Byelorussian and Transcaucasian Republics on 30 December the same year. The republics came together on account of the imperialist dangers posed by Western capitalist powers to destabilize socialism as demonstrated by the preceding four-year long Civil War. In 1940, the USSR grew in size to accommodate eleven more republics including those of the Baltic States. All these countries were constitutionally given the right to join and secede from the Union at will.

The 1936 Constitution of the Soviet Union recognized the leading role of the Communist Party of the Soviet Union in the administration of the Empire.

The Good Samaritan:

Gorbachev in 1986 openly repudiated the Brezhnev Doctrine. This act combined with glasnost and perestroika changed the face of the USSR within months. The reforms were two dimensional- both political and economic. The latter meant increased autonomy for state-owned departments which included allowance for mutual interaction between themselves, relaxation of production targets set by Central policymakers, creation of co-operative societies following Tito's Yugoslavian model, unionization of the workforce to facilitate collective bargaining, incentive-based wage system to increase productivity and some more liberalizing measures most of which were simply not part of the Soviet system since its inception. These ideas to revive the economy to meet increased demand for consumer goods looked rational but extremely insufficient. It must also be noted that Gorbachev, as he is often perceived to be was not a 'free marketeer' but a socialist reformer deeply committed towards bettering the lives of his citizens. The economic reform did grow a lot of detractors internally within the party who were afraid of a departure from the Marxist principles of 'planned economy' but soon they were replaced by Gorbachev with those who toed his line obediently.

But the youngest Head of the Soviet State could not be mistaken for his economic reform which was a good step in the right direction even if it had plenty of limitations. It was only his radical effort to 'politically' reform the Union that ended up spelling great trouble for the Revolution and its founding ideas. His political reform called for greater transparency and accountability which were simply anathema to many of the party bosses and bureaucrats. His path-breaking effort to allow criticism inside the Union and to open the ears of the country to outside led to unforeseen consequences. For the first time, independent presses sprang up all over the Union and foreign media were allowed to report to and outside the Union. This move had deeply undermined the state propaganda discourse which had successfully for decades maintained the great illusion that the Union was doing much better than the rest of the world in almost all indices. News channels soon started reporting the scams and shenanigans of the local bureaucrats and allowed critics to use their platforms to voice dissent which included uncovering the grave crimes committed by the Union's past leaders and the horrible cover-ups that followed. This was undeniably a great shock for the average Russian whose patriotism to his Fatherland was deeply linked to favorable opinions about his iconic leaders. Add to this the culture shock endured by the Russians at the hands of foreign television which narrated stories of Westerners living much more luxurious and freer lives than their own. But that was not the worst of all.

Moscow's sudden shift towards a liberal attitude confused the party leaders in other parts of the Union. Ukraine, Armenia, Azerbaijan were for all these years been remote controlled by Moscow but the leaderships of these countries found their hands suddenly untangled by Gorbachev's reform. The long denied freedom of speech and the right to dissent strengthened the nationalist elements in these countries which began to make their bid for power taking on a weak local Communist leadership which had no help from Moscow all of a sudden. Gorbachev was apprised of these unforeseen developments and he strongly refused to make efforts towards curtailing their momentum. The young leader, if anything was simply walking his talk and behaving like a true socialist. The Soviet constitution had recognized the republics' right to secede from the Union and soon it was left to the leaders of these countries to handle rising nationalist sentiments. Within a year or two, the bigger constituents of the Union were either openly bidding for independence from Moscow or trying to mount spirited resistance against the local anti-reform Communist leadership.

The Union goes to polls:

Gorbachev's sights on foreign policy were clear and unimpeded by the deeds of his predecessors. The Oil shock experienced by the Union in 1985 had crippled the economy and prompted Russian withdrawal from Afghanistan. The Moscow leader had decided not only to de-escalate tensions with its archrival in Washington but also to strike a deal with them irrespective of the cost it entailed. Most of his efforts towards disarmament were unilateral and soon Reagan's successor George Bush of the US was floored by Gorbachev's commitment towards peace and friendship. He impressed the West greatly when he let go of East Germany in 1989 allowing the Berlin Wall to fall signaling the end of the fifty-year old Cold War with the US. This helped Gorbachev to demobilize the Red Army considerably and divert the resources earmarked for military expenses towards increasing industrial productivity.

But from the beginning of 1989, Gorbachev slowly began to recognize the consequences that followed his decision to open up the Union. The anti-reform camp inside the CPSU did everything in their power to block him but Gorbachev resisted them with newer ideas. He in 1989 weakened the Politburo by bringing the party to rubber-stamp his proposal for the creation of a new Congress of People's Deputies. The Congress was supposed to house 2250 deputies elected through direct polls who were in turn allowed to elect the Supreme Soviet headed by the new President. The Union went to elections in March 1989 and Gorbachev's camp won a massive victory in spite of people's declining faith in him making him the first President of the USSR (that included Russia and fourteen other republics).

Even though Gorbachev's efforts towards democratizing the Union looked laudable, various commentators from across the world were accusing him of entrusting himself with so many powers as the President the USSR thereby undermining other organs of the party. This accusation looks true in the face of so much evidence where the new President was found either pig-headed or unrepentant over the repercussions of his reform. He failed to take advice from old, yet sensible hardliners who advocated reform in a carefully planned and phased manner. He refused to listen to the anti-reform camp even on legitimate issues such as the deleterious effects his reform had created on the economy. His anti-alcohol drive which resulted in huge revenue losses had damaged the economic health of the Union and created a huge black market for contraband spirit. The State was not able to support subsidized food products due to declining revenues and hence prices rose which in turn was not accompanied by corresponding wage revisions. Strikes broke across various parts of the Union which were exploited to the hilt by dissenting nationalist elements. Many economists, in retrospect lambast the deficiencies of Gorbachev's spirited economic agenda for having drifted away from the principles of economic planning without adequately laying the foundations for an alternative, workable, market-socialist framework well in advance, something which China devised quite effectively. Consequently the economic reform was neither here nor there earning the wrath of both conservative and reformist elements within the party.

In October 1989, the newly created Supreme Soviet voted to remove reserved seats for the CPSU in national and local elections terming the reservations as wholly 'undemocratic'. It was a historic decision that violated the Soviet Constitution which emphasized the leading role of the Communist Party in the Union's administration. In December 1989, the Supreme Soviet voted in favor of holding direct elections in each of the fifteen constituent republics much to the alarm of Gorbachev.

The year 1989 was a defining year in Soviet history that saw a surge of nationalist demonstrations and clashes in its various constituent republics. Gorbachev by this time in spite of having won power through popular elections began to show signs of incompetence in managing these struggles. He responded sometimes through military and sometimes through conciliatory means which sucked all public confidence in him. The direct elections held in 1990 across the Union led to the defeat of the CPSU in Georgia, Armenia, Latvia, Lithuania, Moldova and Estonia which immediately chose the path of independence from the Union.

The USSR without Russia:

In 1985, Boris Yeltsin was invited by Gorbachev to take over the party functions in the Russian capital. Yeltsin was selected on the basis of his reformist predilections and was soon inducted into the Politburo for his work. Though often called boorish and garrulous by many of his colleagues, Boris was known for his pulse on the masses. He often overstepped his limits by reaching out to the people on his own and his popularity came in good stead for his quick elevation to the top. It is known reliably that his personal ambitions to power were quickly divined by the top brass and his manipulative behavior came up for criticism quite often. The young Mayor of Moscow soon resigned from his position in the Politburo in 1987 after heavily criticizing Gorbachev directly at a Central Committee meeting.

Soon Yeltsin's brave speech in the Central Committee chastising Gorbachev was printed and circulated across the country which did a great deal to establish him as a strong anti-establishment figure within the CPSU who had the unusual guts to stand up even to the Head of the State in defense of his citizens' rights. Boris accused Gorbachev of slower and weak reforms simultaneously castigating his autocratic tendencies. Meanwhile, worker unrest along with severe shortages of food spread all over the Union. Boris capitalized on the anti-establishment wave and contested Russia's independent elections in 1990. The newly elected Congress of the People's deputies of Russia voted for Boris Yeltsin to head the Supreme Soviet of Russia in May the same year defying Gorbachev's instructions.

The President of the USSR, Gorbachev from now on had to take on the Head of the Russian Republic, Boris Yeltsin- a task which became all the more difficult due to ambiguities with respect to separation of powers between the President of the Union and the Head of the Russian State. To make things worse for Gorbachev, Yeltsin in July 1990 resigned from the CPSU in the party's 28[th]Congress ending communist monopoly in Moscow.

However Gorbachev responded by mooting the idea of holding a referendum all over the remaining Soviet territory over the question of 'the preservation of the USSR with full freedom and rights to individuals of all ethnicities'. On March 12, 1991 more than 80 percent of the citizens participated in the referendum and close to three-fourths voted for the preservation of the USSR and its socialist form of government. This meant that citizens residing in Russia, Ukraine, Byelorussia, Kazakhstan, Azerbaijan, Uzbekistan, Kirghizia, Turkmenistan and Tajikistan republics were in favor of staying inside the Union under socialism. But a wily Yeltsin had managed to hold a parallel referendum the same day on whether to create the post of President of Russia who could be directly elected by the people and hence would enjoy privileges and freedom untrammeled by the influences of legislative councils. Russians voted in favor of it and direct elections to the post of President of Russia were held on June 12, 1991.

Gorbachev nominated Nikolai Ryzhov on behalf of the CPSU while Yeltsin contested as an independent. The plummeting popularity of the Union's President was manifest in the election results with Yeltsin polling 58 percent of the vote beating CPSU's candidate by over 43 percentage points. However, it is to be noted that Yeltsin's campaign for the elections was never premised on a 'free-market' plank and hence people rallied around him merely because they mistook him for a committed 'socialist' reformer.

Yeltsin seized the initiative instantly to oust Gorbachev and the CPSU from the Russian soil. Yeltsin's Russia declared itself independent from the Soviet Union immediately after the results came out.

Goodbye Lenin!

Russia's exit from the Soviet Union which was imminent right from the first, rendered useless the purpose of the Union itself. The other smaller republics had agreed to be part of the Union only with a view to forging a close regional co-operation with a powerful Russia at the centre that could complement each other in times of need. Gorbachev's mismanagement of the situation in the smaller republics and glaring ineffectiveness of the local Communist leaderships on account of power-mongering and infighting exacerbated situations in the regional capitals and the most important towns of the Union.

A desperate Gorbachev sought to restructure the Union along less centralized lines by introducing a new Treaty to preserve it. However, hardliners within the CPSU suddenly proclaimed a state of Emergency in August 1991 and ordered the Red Army to arrest Gorbachev at his dacha to reprimand him for his 'anti- Soviet activities'. The coup was doubtless organized without prior preparation and vision by the conservative faction of the CPSU and failed to rally public support. Yeltsin made use of the situation to criticize the CPSU and its autocratic ways and exhorted Russians to stand up to it. The coup collapsed in less than three days and Gorbachev was set free immediately. The news of the failed coup spread all over the other republics and brought the prestige of the CPSU to a new low.

On December 1, 1991 following Russia's lead, the second largest republic of the Union, Ukraine voted in favour of independence joining the long line of seceding republics. Within a week, the leaders of Russia, Ukraine and Byelorussia (Belarus) assembled at Minsk and signed the Belovezha Accord to officially confirm the demise of the Union of Soviet Socialist Republics at the age of 69. The leaders of the other republics gathered at Alma-Ata to formally dissolve the Union on December 21, 1991.

On Christmas day the same year, Mikhail Gorbachev in a televised address announced his resignation as President of the USSR from Kremlin. The very same day, Russia adopted a statute to rename itself from 'Russian Soviet Federative Socialist Republic' to 'Russian Federation' to assert its divorce from socialism and the Union. After Gorbachev left the Kremlin, the Soviet Flag bearing the famous Hammer and Sickle was lowered and replaced with a tricolor at Moscow.

Post Script

The very next week in 1992, Yeltsin let loose a series of market-oriented economic reforms called The Shock Therapy handed down by a group of economists flying in from the IMF for Russia.

By 1998, it was estimated that the GDP of Russia had fallen below half of what it had been in the climactic phases of the Soviet collapse owing to the introduction of Yeltsin's free-market reforms.

In 2001, a report by economist Steven Rosefielde estimated that over 3 million Russians died prematurely in the last decade on account of the indiscriminate opening up of the Russian economy to external market forces.

References

Homage to Catalonia by George Orwell
Khrushchev by Edward Crankshaw
Khrushchev and Khrushchev by William Taubman
The God That Failed book by Louis Fischer
The Rise and Fall of Communism by Archie Brown
Capital by Karl Marx
Fascism and Social Revolution by Rajni Palme Dutt
The Revolution Betrayed by Leon Trotsky
The Rise and Fall of the Third Reich by William Shirer
How to Change the World: Marx and Marxism
1840-2011 by Eric Hobsbawm
The Origin of Family, Private Property and the State
by Friedrich Engels
The Age of Extremes: The Short Twentieth Century,
1914-1991 by Eric Hobsbawm
Dialectical and Historical Materialism by JV Stalin
Russia after Stalin by Isaac Deutscher
Second Hand Time by Svetlana Alexevitch
The Darker Nations by Vijay Prashad
India After Gandhi by Ramachandra Guha
Pin Thodarum Nizhalin Kural by Jeyamohan